Worship:
The Pattern of
Things in Heaven

GENESIS MUSIC WORLD
Christian Music & Literature
4392 Palm Bch. Blvd.- Ft. Myers, FL 33905
(941) 694-7738

Worship:
The Pattern of
Things in Heaven

Joseph L. Garlington

Destiny Image® Publishers, Inc.
P.O. Box 310
Shippensburg, PA 17257-0310

"Speaking to the Purposes of God for This Generation
and for the Generations to Come"

ISBN 1-56043-195-4

For Worldwide Distribution
Printed in the U.S.A.

Fifth Printing: 1999   Sixth Printing: 2000

This book and all other Destiny Image, Revival Press, Mercy Place, Fresh Bread, and Treasure House books are available at Christian bookstores and distributors worldwide.

For a U.S. bookstore nearest you, call **1-800-722-6774**.
For more information on foreign distributors,
call **717-532-3040**.
Or reach us on the Internet: **http://www.reapernet.com**

Dedication

When I call to remembrance the unfeigned faith that is in thee, which dwelt first in thy grandmother Lois, and thy mother Eunice; and I am persuaded that in thee also (2 Timothy 1:5 KJV).

I dedicate this book to my mother, Valdese Garlington—more widely known as "Muttie." She has been my mentor, teacher, and model for worship all my life. Thanks, Mom!

Contents

Foreword

"A promise keeper is committed to honor Jesus Christ through worship, prayer, and obedience to His Word in the power of the Holy Spirit."

As Promise Number One of the Seven Promises of a Promise Keeper indicates, we believe worship is one of the primary disciplines of the Christian life, and, as anyone who's been to a PK conference knows, worship is *central* to what we do. Our stadium events begin with, are punctuated by, and end with "psalms, hymns, and spiritual songs." For many men, it represents the first time they have experienced the true joy of "singing and making melody in their hearts to the Lord" (see Eph. 5:19). It's a worship experience that often ushers them into the very presence of Almighty God. Guys who haven't cried for years (or ever!) find themselves weeping as their hearts overflow with a holy desire to love and obey God more.

True worship is not just an emotional experience. It reaches to the very depths of our souls and touches every aspect of our being. While it can generate powerful feelings, it also can enlighten our minds, expanding our perspective and understanding of God. It can convict us of sin and lead us to repent; it can confirm a Scripture or specific word the Lord may have spoken to us and encourage us to obey; and it can change our hearts and inspire us to reach for new heights of holiness. Such is the power of the sincere praise and adoration of our heavenly Father—and that's just what it does for *us*!

The truly miraculous thing about worship is that in some mysterious way, it also has the power to move the heart of God. It may just be impossible for us to touch Him without it. As the psalmist admonishes, "Worship the Lord with gladness; come before Him with joyful songs. Enter His gates with thanksgiving and His courts with praise; give thanks to Him and praise His name" (Ps. 100:2,4 NIV). In a very real sense, the Almighty receives us on the basis of our worship and thanksgiving. It's our "passage way" into the very throne room of God. As with prayer, the Lord responds to our worship. As we draw near to Him in song, He draws near to us. And as we minister to Him in worship, He ministers to us. As we express faith in Him through praise, He blesses us.

I know few men who understand these things better or who know how to worship God in "spirit and truth" more than Joseph L. Garlington. As a worship leader for Promise Keepers' conferences, Joseph has led hundreds of thousands of men in worshiping the Lord. Whether it's an unusual sensitivity to the Spirit of God or a rare gift, time after time, we've noticed that something special takes place as Joseph directs men in praise to our God. I've seen huge arenas with guys united in joyful (or solemn) worship as he leads them. In response to a call from Joseph, I've also witnessed thousands of men flood a stadium floor, singing from their hearts, lingering in God's Presence and content to go on worshiping indefinitely. That's the effect a godly worship leader can bring to a gathering, whether it's 50,000 men in a football stadium or a home Bible study with just a few people.

I believe Joseph's book, *Worship: The Pattern of Things in Heaven*, offers a wealth of insights on the nature of worship to anyone who reads it. As you consider the perspectives of a man who has become one of the preeminent praise leaders of our time, I pray you'll be encouraged to pursue God with fresh passion and an undivided heart, and that they will inspire in you a holy desire to reach for a deeper level in your worship of our Lord and Savior, Jesus Christ. All glory to His name, now and forevermore!

Bill McCartney
Founder and CEO of Promise Keepers

Introduction

I can't remember a time when music was not a part of my life. My mother, who is still the most passionate worshiper I know, always has been a lover of music. She is an accomplished musician and composer who has trained many choirs and small groups. All of them, it seems, used to come to our tiny apartment in the Willert Park Housing Project in Buffalo, New York, and rehearse. The saying goes, "It's better caught than taught." Whatever she had then, I have now.

I can remember how much music could console my disappointment and keep me entertained when I was alone. When the disciples asked Jesus for an example of a true Kingdom person, He placed before them a child. I don't believe that genuine worship, such that pleases the Father, is possible without "becoming" childlike. When I observe the "little worshipers" in our church and in my family, the attribute that is most apparent to me is the absence of self-consciousness. Children don't become self-conscious until they realize someone is watching them.

"Whatever you do, do heartily as unto the Lord," the apostle Paul told the Colossians (see Col. 3:23). The model worshiper for me is David. I identify with him in so many ways. And, some of the most powerful pictures of his worship are at the two extremes of celebration on the one hand

and great loss on the other. David's description of a sacrifice offered to God is capsulated in his declaration to Araunah the Gibeonite. "However, the king said to Araunah, 'No, but I will surely buy it from you for a price, for I will not offer burnt offerings to the Lord my God which cost me nothing' " (2 Sam. 24:24). I am convinced that, eventually, true worship will "cost" you something. It will cost you your dignity or your self-respect or some other thing you cherish—usually in the sight of others. My suspicion is that we cloak our pride or embarrassment in the kind of words I've heard since I was a child: "It doesn't take *all of that* to please God." But David was different. His attitude seemed to be: "whatever it takes."

Jesus told the Samaritan woman that "the Father seeks" true worshipers. This makes David's passion all the more appealing to me because the prophet Samuel told King Saul, "The Lord has sought out for Himself a man after His own heart" (1 Sam. 13:14). It would be simpler to "find" the Father, if we only would worship.

"Unless you become like a little child," Jesus said. I have learned that "becoming" is a process, and that is especially true of becoming a worshiper. That "becoming" process will be the same for you and me as it was for King David. What it eventually will mean is that the more mature I become in worship, the more childlike I will be in the presence of the Ancient of Days. In fact, David told his wife Michal that he would continue to "play before the Lord." His own sense of identity is insignificant compared to his regard for his Creator. I want to be just like that.

"We had fun in church today!" These were the words of an eight-year-old expressing her delight for an incredible time of worship that touched every generation. A friend of mine in our city who pastors a mainline denominational church visited our services one summer. He told me later that his son said, "Dad, this is a fun church. Why don't we come here on Sundays?" Covenant Church of Pittsburgh has a purpose statement that attempts to capture our reason for existence. A portion reads: "Covenant Church of Pittsburgh exists to glorify God through a proper response to the Lordship of Jesus Christ; to express that response through wholehearted obedience to the scriptures, powerful worship...."

Our church is involved in many endeavors in our city. We are reaching out to the community in many different ways, and our burden over the years is to be a credible model of the message of reconciliation. If you were to ask the average person in our region what we are known for, however, the response you would invariably hear is "the worship." There are two phrases from the movie *The Field of Dreams* that have impacted me in my approach to church growth. The first is the most quoted one: "If you build it, he will come." The second is at the end of the movie after he has built it, and it seems to be in vain. His little daughter says, "People will come."

David said in Psalm 22, verse 3, that God inhabits the praises of His people. A few years ago, while I was ministering in Japan, one of the pastors said that a translation of that passage in Japanese was: "When we worship, we build a big chair for Him to come and sit in." Well, that is what we've been doing at Covenant for the past decade—and more. My conviction is simply this: If He comes, He will bring or cause to come anyone and everyone who is hungry for His Presence. Our church is in an "inner city" section of a suburb of Pittsburgh, called Wilkinsburg. Our services are packed every Sunday. We have a terrible parking problem and times of street violence. Our budget includes regular security for our worshipers, yet still, we grow. We grow in violation of almost every church growth "rule" that I know. We have three services, congestion, and all the other harrowing issues of exhausted resources. Still, they come. They come from every race, every economic background, and every generation.

Worship for us is the primary thing. We have invested in it; we constantly see the dividends. Five of our full-time staff persons primarily are involved in worship. We have two part-time staff persons in the music ministry. We are committed to writing, recording, composing, and spreading this message. The concepts and principles of this book are the result of a lifetime of study and a wonderful church family that has been willing to be a "laboratory" for the development of these ideas.

It is my hope that you will find some new truths falling into your hands or some old truths made fresh by the quickening work of the Holy Spirit. And may we, the Church of Jesus Christ, come to know from experience what the creed declares when it says, "The chief end of man is to glorify God and enjoy Him forever."

It is my prayer that you will find new paradigms of worship and praise as you join me in participating in *Worship: The Pattern of Things in Heaven*. As you do, we will join an eternal stream of worshipers who have continued since their creation till now. "You've come to Mount Zion, the city where the living God resides. The invisible Jerusalem is populated by throngs of festive angels and Christian citizens" (Heb. 12:22 The Message).

Part I

I Love to Worship You, Lord!

Chapter 1

I Love to Worship You, Lord!

But an hour is coming, and now is, when the true worshipers shall worship the Father in spirit and truth; ***for such people the Father seeks to be His worshipers*** (John 4:23).

Jesus was talking to a divorced woman of questionable character and mixed race beside a well in Samaria nearly two thousand years ago when He shared a powerful secret: His Father is seeking people to be His worshipers. I think we need to return to the well and hear Jesus speak those words again. How does your "New Testament" church experience compare to what Jesus described to the woman at the well? The ideal answer would be this: "It's a perfect match! We exist to worship Him morning, noon, and night. When we come together, we come to praise and worship Him with all of our hearts, all of our souls, all of our minds, and all of our strength! He always meets us there."

Honestly, how would you describe "God's desire" if the only evidence you could draw from was your home church and your personal life? (That's all the unsaved have to work with!) I am afraid that some of us would have to say:

"I think God is looking for the most fashionable and conservative people to gather in His name once a week in a sad, solemn assembly."

"I think God is looking for people who just come to church to have a good time and get blessed."

"I think God is looking for an audience of patient people so His preachers will have someone to preach at."

"It looks like God is looking for bored people who like to dress up and wait around at the church until it's time to eat lunch at noon, especially on Sundays."

This is pretty serious when you consider what God says about His desire (worship) in the Old Testament. "And it will be that whichever of the families of the earth does not go up to Jerusalem *to worship* the King, the Lord of hosts, *there will be no rain on them*" (Zech. 14:17).

God says, "No worship, no rain." One of the reasons I love to worship so much is because I appreciate rain. When you realize that certain necessary things are *conditional* upon your response to God, you will learn to adjust your response to God appropriately. Our congregation is reminded of our proper response to God every time they look at a church bulletin. We've printed it in plain view for everyone to see: "Covenant Church of Pittsburgh exists to glorify God through a proper response to the Lordship of Jesus Christ; to express that response through wholehearted obedience to the scriptures, powerful worship...."

You may have noticed that we didn't say "powerful singing." That is because you can have powerful singing that is not powerful worship. Mr. Luciano Pavarotti is a powerful opera singer, but that is not what worship is. Worship is "powerful" inasmuch as we understand the dynamics that take place when it is going on.

Do you remember the Bible account in the third chapter of the Book of Joshua when the Levite priests were asked to carry the ark of the covenant across the River Jordan at the height of the harvest floods? God said: "And it shall come about when the soles of the feet of the priests who carry the ark of the Lord...shall rest in the waters of the Jordan, the waters of the Jordan shall be cut off, and the waters which are flowing down from above shall stand in one heap" (Josh. 3:13).

God was telling Joshua, "Now while you are stepping into the water right here, I am going to cut off the current upstream way up there, far from your view." When you and I walk in obedience and do our part, God always does His part—but you usually won't see what God does behind the scenes. You will only see what *you* have done most of the time. And if you happen to find yourself wading through a raging river at harvest time with only His promise to cling to, then you might catch yourself wondering if God has really done His part. Worship is like that. When I am worshiping, I'm not always aware of what God is doing because my focus is centered on what I am doing. Worship is my faith response to God.

Now *worship* is almost always confused with *praise*, even by people who ought to know better. Worship doesn't mean "to lift your hands." That is actually a loose definition of praise. There are 12 different Hebrew and Greek words translated as *worship* in the Bible. All four of the Hebrew words, and especially the primary word *shachah*, mean "to depress, prostrate (in homage to royalty or God)—bow down, crouch, fall down (flat), humbly beseech, do (make) obeisance, do reverence, make to stoop, worship."[1]

To worship is to act as an inferior before a superior. When I worship God, I am saying by my actions, "God, You are better than I am. You are bigger than I am. You are more than I am." We sing the song, "Our God is an *awesome* God," but our understanding of those words is clouded by our misuse and abuse of the word *awesome* in everyday life. We use "awesome" to describe everything from our favorite sports team, movie star, or musician to our favorite flavor of ice cream. If we say "tutti-frutti" ice cream and God are both awesome, then it is obvious that we don't understand the meaning of *awesome*. Somehow it doesn't seem accurate to use the same word to describe our God as we do our favorite high-fat food.

We worship God because He truly is awesome. His very Presence inspires awe. When you recognize God's awesomeness, it will evoke a certain response from you because you see something and Someone who is different and higher than you are. You know instantly and instinctively that you are in the presence of One who is worthy of more honor than you are. It is this awe that inspires you to worship He who is greater than you and every other man and woman before you.

As you read through the Scriptures, you will find people worshiping God at some of the strangest times. We need to understand why this happens. If we don't understand worship, if we don't create a love for worship in our hearts, then according to God's Word, we aren't going to get any rain in our land!

To fully appreciate the importance of God's words in Zechariah, you need to understand where God's people were coming from and where they were going to when this prophecy was given. God made a clear distinction between Egypt, the land of bondage, and the promised land, Canaan:

> *For the land, into which you are entering to possess it, is not like the land of Egypt from which you came, where you used to sow your seed and **water it with your foot** like a vegetable garden.*

> *But the land into which you are about to cross to possess it, a land of hills and valleys, **drinks water from the rain of heaven,***

> *A land for which the Lord your God cares; the eyes of the Lord your God are always on it, from the beginning even to the end of the year.*

And it shall come about, if you listen obediently to my commandments which I am commanding you today, to love the Lord your God and to serve Him with all your heart and all your soul,

That **He will give the rain** *for your land in its season, the early and late rain, that you may gather in your grain and your new wine and your oil* (Deuteronomy 11:10-14).

Even today, Egypt is still essentially a parched land of canals linked with its life-source, the Nile River. The great Aswan Dam project completed several decades ago was Egypt's modern attempt to tame the Nile and reduce the nation's dependence on that river. In Bible times, there was no Aswan Dam to help regulate the river's fluctuations. Farmers watered small patches of land artificially with foot-powered primitive pumps constructed beside the river or its canals. A foot lever attached to a boom with a bucket or paddle dipped small amounts of water out of the river or canal and into the flat fields of that region.

Then, as now, things are different in God's promised land of lush hills and fertile valleys. Here, God Himself sovereignly sends rain from heaven to water the land and preserve the life and productivity of His people. But it comes with a warning: "As long as you do right, you'll get rain. If you don't, then there will come a time when the heavens will be to you as brass, and the ground will be to you as dust" (see Deut. 11:10-14; 28:23-24).

Do you remember what God told Solomon one night after the dedication of the temple? He said, "[If] My people who are called by My name humble themselves and pray, and seek My face and turn from their wicked ways, then I will hear from heaven, will forgive their sin, and will heal their land" (2 Chron. 7:14). The word *humble* is actually *kana',* one of the four Hebrew words for *worship* in the Old Testament. It means "to bend the knee; hence to humiliate, vanquish:—bring down (low), into subjection, under, humble (self), subdue."[2] Remember that while *praise* speaks of hands extended to God, *worship* speaks of bent knees and bowed faces pressed to the ground in His awesome Presence.

Now when you say "hear from heaven" in a land that depends on rain for survival, there is only one thing you want to hear from heaven: *thunder.* You long to hear from something that says, "The rain is coming!"

What is worship? It is the ability to look at God and bow yourself before His will—even in the face of what seems to be certain disaster. Whether you realize it or not, everything about your life is dependent upon your ability to say, "My God is an awesome God."

When you get bad news that seems to discount your promise from God, do you pretend that you didn't and say: "Hurting? Oh no, praise God! Amen, yes I'm blessed, brother"? Even though you're hurting like crazy, do you pretend that you aren't and privately wonder: *There's something wrong here! Something wacky is going on because if God had really given me this promise, and if He was really doing what He promised He would do, then why in the world has God put me in this predicament?*

Not only is worship the response of faith in the face of disaster, but it is also the response of faith to the success of the blessed. Worship is something you should do *all the time,* not just when things are going great or going terribly. We should always be worshipers because we always have a reason to worship.

Let me tell you right now that if you're waiting until you get to church to worship, then you're missing most of your worship time! Jesus recited the greatest commandment this way: "You shall love the Lord your God with all your heart, and with all your soul, and with all your mind" (Mt. 22:37). I know many of us are tempted to say, "That's right! I worship

God with all of my heart for a solid two-and-a-half hours every single Sunday morning service at First Church!" No, Jesus was talking about a daily thing, a weekly thing. David, the greatest worshiper and psalmist among men, said he offered morning and evening sacrifices, along with even more times of worship for a minimum of seven times a day! (See Psalm 119:164.) Worship is like breathing: You were created to do it all the time. It's a lifestyle.

When everything imaginable comes against you, worship God. When things finally go your way, worship Him. (Of course, it's easier to worship in the good times.) Nothing else will be as creative as worship, because you are doing more than expressing faith in the sovereign God. You are *creating an atmosphere* in your own heart and circumstances that releases faith and enables you to say, "My God is in control of this." Worshiping allows you to get in touch with a "higher reason" than not worshiping.

Too many of us get excited and agitated when God asks us to give up something that He gave us in the first place. Now if God asks you to give it up, give it up! But you might as well give it up while you've got your hands in the air in praise and surrender. Let the incense of your prayers be as an evening sacrifice. Let your obedience be something that is sweet in the nostrils of God. Tell the Lord the truth. "Well Lord, I'm here. I don't understand what You told me to do, and I can't seem to figure it out. But I do have this much figured out: You've got an answer that I can't see."

If you knew you were about to be laid off, would you say, "I'm going to go worship"? That's what faith says. Look, even if it is your fault that you got fired, you can still worship Him and take a stand on Romans 8:28, "And we know that God causes all things to work together for good to those who love God, to those who are called according to His purpose."

There are so many places in the Scriptures that inspire and trigger worship that you shouldn't have a problem with worshiping any time or any hour of the day. If you're confused, find the passage that says, "God is not the author of confusion," and worship right there (see 1 Cor. 14:33). When you worship, you're saying: "God, You're better than I am. You know more than I know. You've got it all laid out. I don't understand it. I messed up, but so did David, and he was a man after Your own heart. I'm going to worship You, Lord. I didn't worship before, and that's why I'm in this predicament, but I'm going to worship You now."

When you worship, you are prostrating yourself before God. You are submitting your intellect, your future, and your arrogance to God. You are literally submitting your sense of superiority to God. You may not understand your circumstances or God's commands, but you need to start saying: "Lord God, I've got my hands in the air, I've got my face bowed before You, and I'm resisting questions. The enemy is attacking me with all kinds of signals and doubting thoughts, but I'm not dealing with any of that. I've got my hands up and my mouth open wide so I can worship and praise You, Lord. I'm worshiping You. I'm celebrating the reality that my God is an awesome God."

It is important for us to remember that God never said you would understand Him. Scripture does not say, "You shall *understand* the Lord your God with all your *mind*." No, it says, "You shall *love* the Lord your God with all your heart, and with all your soul, and with all your mind" (Mt. 22:37). This is what you and I were created to do. We will never be able to "figure Him out" because He dwells in unapproachable light and no mortal man can approach Him there (see 1 Tim. 6:16). He is inscrutable, immutable. He discloses Himself to us when, where, and how He chooses; and when He doesn't want us to see Him, He hides Himself in His glory. Either way, the only choice He puts before you is to "come and worship Me."

Endnotes

1. James Strong, *Strong's Exhaustive Concordance of the Bible* (Peabody, Massachusetts: Hendrickson Publishers, n.d.), **worship** (H7812). (These meanings are drawn from their prime root words and so may not be exact to *Strong's*.)

2. *Strong's*, **humble** (H3665).

Chapter 2

The Art of Altar Building

I have been told that long ago potters used to put their earthenware vases in ovens to temper them as we do now. They had one major problem, however. Since they didn't have clocks or all of the technical gear we have today, they had to literally "play it by ear." One man watched a potter work on his vessel, and when the artisan put it in the oven, the observer asked, "How long will you leave it in there?"

The potter straightened up and said, "Some take longer than others, and some not so long. It just depends on how I make the piece. You see, we never make them just alike."

"Well, how do you know when it's done?" the man asked.

The potter shrugged and said, "We keep it in the heat until it sings."

The surprised observer said, "What do you mean, 'Until it sings'?"

Patiently the potter explained, "There is a noise that emanates from tempered pottery in the heat of a furnace once it reaches the proper heat point. When we hear the pottery 'singing' in the furnace, we know it's ready to be removed from the heat. Stay right here, and listen for the song."

So the man sat there by the oven while the potter returned to his potter's wheel. Sure enough, after a short time he began to hear a high-pitched hum coming from the oven. The man glanced at the potter and said, "Is it singing now?"

The potter nodded and said, "It sure is. It's fully tempered and ready to come out."

You may be in the midst of your own fire right now! Let me ask you this: "Are you singing yet?" We need to learn how to sing when we are being heated in what the Bible calls "the furnace of affliction" (see Is. 48:10). There is a song that goes, "For in the furnace of My affliction, I have chosen thee, Behold/And so for iron I'll give you silver, and for brass I'll give you gold/Awake O Israel, put on your garments..../For You are glorious, and worthy to be praised, O Lamb upon the throne...." Pray this prayer out loud with me:

> *Lord, we want to learn how to worship You, and how to experience the meaning of worship in our own lives. Not just here in this place, or in other places like it, but everywhere. You are not confined to a building. You are not confined to rooms that have a gathering of Christians who worship You. No, You dwell in our hearts, and You are a spirit. Those who worship You must worship You in spirit and in truth, and we want to do that today. We worship You, Lord. Amen.*

We need to learn more about what worship is, because God has created us to worship Him. This is an "interactive" message, and you are part of it. Don't be surprised if you find yourself laying this book down from time to time so you can practice what you are learning about worship. If I have done my job, then you should be sensing the gentle nudge of the Holy Spirit calling you to worship every time you read a major passage in this book!

One of the most difficult things to grasp about worship is its unique connection to suffering, affliction, and adversity. No, active worship won't necessarily bring these things to your life, but it will always be enriched and deepened by these circumstances. And every time, God uses hard times to perfect, strengthen, and cleanse us—even though He isn't the source of your pain. One way to get a healthy perspective on suffering is to consider this passage in the Book of Hebrews:

Although He was a Son, He learned obedience from the things which He suffered.

And having been made perfect, He became to all those who obey Him the source of eternal salvation (Hebrews 5:8-9).

We are created to praise Him, to worship Him. With that in mind, do you understand that obedience is the highest form of worship you can offer to God? In fact, when obedience is absent from your relationship with God, none of the other forms of sacrifice, thanksgiving, or worship will have enough value to cover your disobedience. King Saul found this out the hard way. God told him through Samuel the prophet, "Has the Lord as much delight in burnt offerings and sacrifices as in obeying the voice of the Lord? Behold, to obey is better than sacrifice, and to heed than the fat of rams" (1 Sam. 15:22).

When King David committed adultery with Bathsheba and then plotted her husband's murder to cover his sin, God confronted him through Nathan the prophet and said, "Your baby is going to die" (see 2 Sam. 12:15). David went into fasting and prayer and prostrated himself on his face before God. Seven days later he heard the servants whispering and he knew his son was dead. Then David did something that his servants thought was odd: He got up, cleaned himself up, and went into the house of the Lord, and he worshiped (see 2 Sam. 12:20).

When you are in the heat of the furnace of affliction, the only thing you can do that has any substance, any value, or any creative power at all, is to worship! Why? Scripture says, "Yet Thou art holy, O Thou who art *enthroned upon the praises* of Israel" (Ps. 22:3).

I think every living thing has a particular environment in which it excels. The eagle excels in the air because that's the eagle's environment. The dolphin excels in the sea because that's the environment of the dolphin. The cheetah excels on the ground, reaching speeds of 60 miles an hour because it was created to be a running machine!

God excels in an atmosphere permeated by worship and praise. When you worship Him, He gets excited. Paul and Silas were beaten and thrown in jail for preaching the gospel, and God was in Heaven minding His business in Acts 16:25. Then Paul and Silas started singing songs and hymns and spiritual songs in the darkest hour of their pain and isolation. Even though their bodies ached and their feet were still painfully confined in stocks, they filled the dark shadows of their jail cell at midnight by singing at the top of their lungs to the glory of God. As the sound of their praise and worship filled that cell in the heart of the jail, the other prisoners locked inside that miserable place began to listen to them, and suddenly *the atmosphere began to change.*

You can change the atmosphere where you are, too, *if you will worship Him.* I doubt that you will ever find yourself in a worse situation than the kind Paul and Silas faced that dreary night in Thyatira, but if you do, you need to begin to worship and sing to the Lord like they did. Why? Because God will hear you. I can almost hear Him telling the angels and His Son, "I'm going down there, I'm going to wear earthquake shoes, and I'm going to introduce myself to those jailers." When those men began to sing God's praises and worship Him, God looked down and said, "I'm coming, I'm coming, because I like what I hear."

When you find yourself in the middle of trials and tribulations, it sounds a lot better to God when you sing or pray, "I worship You, Lord. I bless Your holy name. I glorify You," rather than when you whine and moan, "Lord, why is all this happening to me?"

I'm sure you know someone who makes you want to hide every time you see him coming because you know he's going to complain and whine the moment he sees you. You want to hide because you are not thrilled to listen to someone else's complaints. God isn't either. God delights in our praise and our worship.

It is during the dark moments that you need to remind yourself, "Lord, You haven't lost track of me, and when You're done with me, when You're done testing me, I'm going to come forth as gold."

Most of us want rain in our lives, but we're not going to get it unless we understand that rain is the product of a faithful and abiding relationship with God. The best source of instruction for godly worship is God's Word, the "Manufacturer's Handbook." You may not be a farmer, but I think you realize that "rain from Heaven" refers to God's blessing and provision—the essence of your survival. Just as rain is important to the land, the Presence of God is vitally important to us. We cannot make it without Him. God says, "No worship, no rain."

The origins of the English word *worship* give us some insight into the original Hebrew term as well. *Worship* comes from the Anglo-Saxon compound word, *weorthscype*. (It is as hard to pronounce as it looks.) The first part of this word, *weorth*, speaks of "worth, value, or respect." The second part, *-scype* or *-scipe*, meant "to shape or to build something." When the two parts were combined into *weorthscype*, it formed a word which meant "to shape or build worth, value, or respect." Since language tends to devolve or degenerate over time, the original meaning of this word gradually has changed over the centuries.

In England, and in other countries which still maintain a monarchy or social system of royalty, the citizens have an innate understanding of words like *worship, lord, king,* and *kingdom.* Americans, however, suffer a distinct disadvantage in this area. The word *lord* is difficult for most Americans to really understand because we don't have any lords, dukes, duchesses, knights, kings, or queens in our social and political system. When we're talking about the Lordship of Jesus Christ to people in representative democratic societies, we have to begin with a definition of *lordship.* When the translators of the King James Bible translated the Greek word *kurios* as "Lord," they had reason for doing so. They had an earthly king and a whole collection of lords and ladies to honor and respect. Americans don't even use the word *lord* outside of the church or the movie theater.

When you talk about the Lordship of Jesus Christ, you're talking about somebody who says, "Your very existence depends upon Me." So when we offer worship to such an all-powerful being, even the posture of our body and the words of our mouths should frame the worth, value, and respect due to His name and person. Another root of "ship" in *weorthscype* is *scip,* or "ship." When we offer worship to God, we literally become vessels or ships immersed in His infinite worth and value.

That leads me to the art of altar building and our spiritual father of faith, Abraham. This converted moon-worshiper, who became the first great worshiper of God since Noah, left us an example of worship as a lifestyle that we need to heed today. As you read through the short verses below, you should notice something unique about the life of Abraham:

*And the Lord appeared to Abram and said, "To your descendants I will give this land." So he **built an altar there to the Lord** who had appeared to him.*

Then he proceeded from there to the mountain on the east of Bethel, and pitched his tent, with Bethel on the west and Ai on the east; and **there he built an altar to the Lord** *and called upon the name of the Lord* (Genesis 12:7-8).

Then Abram moved his tent and came and dwelt by the oaks of Mamre, which are in Hebron, and **there he built an altar to the Lord** (Genesis 13:18).

So "there he built an altar." Abraham was constantly building altars to the Lord, and God was constantly meeting him and confirming His promises and provision to him. Do you think we could learn anything from this pattern?

The Hebrew word for altar, *mizbeach*, described a structure that had only one function or reason for existence: the slaughter of sacrifices. We no longer have altars in that sense because Jesus offered Himself once and for all as the supreme sacrifice to take away the sins of the world. Now our altars are spiritual altars, but we still perform vital functions on them. Like Abraham, we actively participate in the building of those altars every time we begin to worship God. Most of us think we are "just singing" or praying on bent knees, but the spiritual reality is that we are shaping, building, and constructing something that is holy unto the Lord.

First we build a throne for our First Love with our praises. Psalm 22:3 says, "Yet Thou art holy, O Thou who art enthroned upon the praises of Israel." God's throne is as significant as we want to make it through our praises. Now if He dwells in the midst of your praises, how much of a throne do you want Him to have?

As you praise Him, you are shaping a throne for God Almighty, Himself, in your life or in the corporate body seeking His face. As you worship Him, you are sacrificing your life and body on an altar of surrender as a living sacrifice. This says to God, "I have confidence that You are the sovereign God of the universe. My whole being leans upon You for life and fullness."

Although Abraham had very little control over the circumstances of his life, he did have a promise, and he knew how to build altars to the living God. In the end, it turned out that he didn't need anything more than the promise, ability, and desire to build altars. Like me, you probably have very little, if any, control over your circumstances. You can't control the gross national product, inflation, foreign oil markets, or the fact that egg prices may go up 20 cents tomorrow. But remember what you *can* control!

You can control the reality of your atmosphere at all times. Any time you choose, you can build a throne for the Lord through your praises, and you can worship your all-powerful God by offering your life on the altar of submission. Your acts of selfless worship to God can create an atmosphere in which He can say, "I want to spend some time with you! I like the throne you have built for Me. I like the way you lavishly put this thing together, and I especially appreciate the living sacrifice you are offering to Me on the altar of sacrifice." True spiritual worship will cause God Almighty to come and sit with you, for He is enthroned in the midst of your praises.

As Abraham moved from one geographical spot to another and set up camp, his mind was on God. If he already had camped at the site before, he already had built an altar to offer sacrifices. If he had never been at a spot before, then the first thing Abraham did was to build a new altar! He pitched his tent, and he built an altar to the Lord.

The Bible says, "You will know them [men] by their fruits" (Mt. 7:20). You can tell at a glance what matters most to Abraham—where he lives with his family and the altar where he worships. He pitches a tent, and he builds an altar. A clear pattern is established in Abraham's life. He is getting "altar building" experience. Now how about you? It is very important for you to learn how to build an altar of worship in your own personal experience. Just as you need to learn how to change a tire in the driveway before you have a flat in the desert, you need to learn how to build an altar of worship to God in the good times before you land in a dark valley with no altar-building experience.

Look closely at what happened later in Abraham's life: "Now it came about after these things, that God *tested* Abraham…" (Gen. 22:1a). The Hebrew word translated as "tested" also means to "assay," which is what you do to gold ore to see if there is really gold hidden in it, and if so, how much. You also *assay* mixed precious metals by heating them to the melting point to separate the precious metals from the common metals and contaminants. *Webster's Dictionary* says the way to judge the worth of something is "to *prove* up in an assay."[1]

God is saying, "Build some altars. Learn the art of altar building." Even if you build a bad one, it's better than building none at all. Why? Because the day will come when God will want to *assay* or test for gold in your life too! The test is coming whether you know it or not. God told Abraham, "Take now your son, your only son, whom you love, Isaac, and go to the land of Moriah; and offer him there as a burnt offering on one of the mountains of which I will tell you" (Gen. 22:2).

The Bible tells us that Abraham arose early the next morning, saddled his donkey, and took his son Isaac and two servants on a journey. First he cut enough wood for the burnt offering; then he headed for Moriah. On the third day he saw his destination in the distance and told his servants to wait with the donkey. Then he said something we need to remember: "…I and the lad will go yonder; and *we will worship and return to you*" (Gen. 22:5b). Are you beginning to understand why this man is often called "the father of faith"?

Abraham loaded all the wood for the burnt offering on Isaac's back, while he carried the coals for the fire and the knife. At some point, Isaac asked, " 'Behold, the fire and the wood, but where is the lamb for the burnt offering?' And Abraham said, 'God will provide for Himself the lamb for the burnt offering, my son' " (Gen. 22:7b-8).

As soon as Abraham reached the place of God's choosing, what did he do? He built an altar and put his bound son on top of the wood. He was determined to carry out God's command and trust Him to make good on His promise somehow. It was only as Abraham reached out for the slaughtering knife and gathered his strength to strike the fatal blow that an angel of God shouted out, "Abraham, Abraham!" (See Genesis 22:11.)

God is going to talk to you some day about something in your life that He wants you to release, confront, or deal with. When He does, you can be sure He will have given you enough time to prepare and learn. God is the fairest and most just of all instructors. He will never give you an "exam" that He knows you're not ready for—*if you've done what you should* with the things He has given you.

When you are perched on Mount Moriah in the crisis of your life, that is no time to pull out the Manufacturer's Handbook and say, "Now, what do I do here? Where do I put this?" God may appear to be doing one of those reverses in your life, but you can't build an altar out of anxiety. Now, if you are a man or woman who has been building altars already—if your whole life has been wrapped up in the godly pattern of pitching a tent and building an altar—then the first thing you will do in a crisis is to build an altar and worship in the presence of God.

The only way to build an altar is to remove your focus from your problem and put it on God and His promises. As an altar builder, you have a tremendous edge in any situation: You know God will meet you whenever you build Him an altar and offer Him praise and worship! David prayed,

"May my prayer be counted as incense before Thee; the lifting up of my hands as the evening offering" (Ps. 141:2). You can build an altar anywhere, and you don't even have to get loud to build it.

The writer of Hebrews tells us that Abraham believed that God was able to raise Isaac from the dead (see Heb. 11:19). He was convinced that God was able to raise up his son's ashes if necessary, but He would keep His promise to Abraham. It is significant that Abraham laid the wood on Isaac, and that this promised son had to carry the burden of the very wood that was going to take his life. Thousands of years later, another only beloved Son would carry rough-hewn wood up the same mountain and offer His life as a sacrifice for many. But three days later....

Has God made you a promise, only to make a demand that apparently will leave you nothing but ashes? Like Abraham, you believe your God is a God who says, "Ashes or no ashes, you are going to have your promise." If you're not building altars now, don't expect to be able to build them later under the pressure of a trial or crisis. Practice glorifying and magnifying Him now. Do you know what you do when you magnify God? You make Him *bigger than the situation* engulfing you.

Start talking about the God who made the heavens and the earth, who put the stars into existence and spoke galaxies into space. Speak of the Creator God who went to work to the joyful accompaniment of His magnificent chorus of angels singing of His glory and wonder.

As you worship Him, He will exceed His own greatness in your life! God isn't locked up somewhere saying, "I wonder if I can beat what I did yesterday?" Paul prays in the Book of Ephesians:

Now to Him who is able to do exceeding abundantly beyond all that we ask or think, according to the power that works within us,

*to Him be the glory in the church and in Christ Jesus to all
generations forever and ever. Amen* (Ephesians 3:20-21).

That's the kind of God you serve. You need to learn how
to praise and worship Him, no matter what is going on or
how much you understand it. Build a throne of praise and
see Him seated as the Lord of your life. And when you hear
bad news, make some good news right there by shaping an
altar of sacrifice through worship before His throne.

When God sees your hands lifted to Him, He sees surrender and adoration. Your prayers create the sweet-smelling
smoke of incense before Him, and when you praise Him, He
sees lambs and calves of sacrifice! The Bible describes the
fruit of our lips as the calves of our mouths. Offer your Creator a sacrifice of praise, and then submit your very life and
body to Him as a living sacrifice of humble, submitted worship. You can be sure that He will join you in the fullness of
His glory and power because you have created an atmosphere in which He always excels.

Endnotes

1. *Merriam Webster's Collegiate Dictionary, 10th Edition*
(Springfield, Massachusetts: Merriam-Webster Inc., 1994),
p. 69.

Chapter 3

What Is the Volume of Heavenly Worship?

Every week of the year, millions of people pass through church doors, dragging with them centuries of religious presumption, assumption, and outright error. About the only thing most of them would agree on is the need to impose their own narrow ideas of what constitutes worship onto everyone else. My question is this: What does God have to say about worship in His Word?

Some of us think we are courting gross error and heresy if we worship God from anything other than an approved church hymnal and the Book of Common Prayer (and yes, there are anointed songs and prayers in them). Others don't think they've "had church" unless they've done cartwheels, blown out the speakers on the sound system, sweat through two sets of church clothes, and received at least two visits from the local constable about the neighbors' public disturbance complaints. Some believers feel that true worship can only issue from the vocal chords of believers, and they shun the use of all instruments or musical accompaniment in their services. Others feel something is missing if there isn't a Hammond B-3 organ, a stack of electronic keyboards with MIDI interfaces, a whole battery of electric guitars, electric bass guitars, and drum sets crowding the stage and spilling out onto the floor of the sanctuary.

What does God think? (You might be surprised.)

If the experiences of King David and King Solomon are any guide, God likes exuberant and elaborate praise with lots of dancing and excitement, and enough instruments to reach every eardrum for miles! Consider the Bible record:

So David and all the house of Israel were bringing up the ark of the Lord with shouting and the sound of the trumpet.

Then it happened as the ark of the Lord came into the city of David that Michal the daughter of Saul looked out of the window and saw King David leaping and dancing before the Lord (2 Samuel 6:15-16a).

When King Solomon dedicated the temple at Jerusalem, the music team and singers included 120 priests blowing trumpets at the top of their lungs; an untold number of musicians playing cymbals, harps, lyres, and new musical instruments specially created by King David for the worship of God; and several generations of Levitical singers from three priestly families:

And all the Levitical singers, Asaph, Heman, Jeduthun, and their sons and kinsmen, clothed in fine linen, with cymbals, harps, and lyres, standing east of the altar, and with them one hundred and twenty priests blowing trumpets

*In unison when the trumpeters and the singers **were to make themselves heard with one voice to praise and to glorify the Lord,** and when they lifted up their voice accompanied by trumpets and cymbals and instruments of music, and when they praised the Lord saying, "He indeed is good for His lovingkindness is everlasting," then the house, **the house of the Lord, was filled with a cloud,***

*So that the priests could not stand to minister because of the cloud, **for the glory of the Lord filled the house of God*** (2 Chronicles 5:12-14).

Years later, David's son Solomon led the nation in a prayer of confession and covenant before God during the dedication of the new temple, and the Lord's public response was even more enthusiastic:

*Now when Solomon had finished praying, **fire came down from heaven** and consumed the burnt offering and the sacrifices; **and the glory of the Lord filled the house.***

And the priests could not enter into the house of the Lord, because the glory of the Lord filled the Lord's house.

*And all the sons of Israel, seeing the fire come down and the glory of the Lord upon the house, **bowed down on the pavement with their faces to the ground, and they worshiped** and gave praise to the Lord, saying, "Truly He is good, truly His lovingkindness is everlasting"* (2 Chronicles 7:1-3).

Although the Bible is filled with rich references to exuberant praise and worship in prostration before God, countless modern church services are begun with the dry recitation of one Scripture verse: "But the Lord is in His holy temple. Let all the earth be silent before Him" (Hab. 2:20). The verse usually is read to the entire congregation by a minister using his most solemn and God-like voice to impress on the people the gravity of the atmosphere. May I say to you that if you were to look for other verses just like this one, you wouldn't find them. This is the only verse in the Bible that says, "The Lord is in His holy temple, so shut up!"

Somehow, this isolated verse has been elevated to the level of a church doctrine or ordinance of operation. The truth is that this verse is almost always quoted with no reference to context. If the readers bothered to read the verses before and after this verse (remember that chapter and verse divisions were added later by a Catholic monk for convenience), they would find this:

Woe to him who says to a piece of wood, "Awake!" To a dumb stone, "Arise!" And that is your teacher? Behold, it is overlaid with gold and silver, and there is no breath at all inside it.

"But the Lord is in His holy temple. Let all the earth be silent before Him."

A prayer of Habakkuk the prophet, according to Shigionoth.

Lord, I have heard the report about Thee and I fear. O Lord, revive Thy work in the midst of the years, in the midst of the years make it known; in wrath remember mercy (Habakkuk 2:19–3:2).

The word *Shigionoth* is thought by many Bible scholars to be a musical or literary term. The editors of the Amplified Bible say it this way: "A prayer of Habakkuk the prophet, set to wild, enthusiastic, and triumphal music" (Hab. 3:1 AMP). Now remember that this verse immediately follows the verse that says, "The Lord is in His holy temple, let all the earth be silent before Him."

"So what are you going to do, Habakkuk?"

"We are going to sing about the wildest song you ever heard in your life—wild, enthusiastic, and triumphal music."

"Why are you going to do that?"

"Because that's what comes next on the program."

Essentially, Habakkuk is telling us to get silent for a moment so we can focus on the One we are going to worship. He also is making a point of saying that we need to be silent at times because, unlike the mute and man-made gods of wood and stone, this God is alive and at home. He speaks to His people! Once we have fixed our focus on Him, we are to worship Him with all of our might and strength! (I don't know about you, but it doesn't take any might or strength at all to sit mute in a pew like a lifeless corpse. It seems more like an imitation of death than worship. I can't help but think of Second Timothy 3:5, which speaks of "having a form of godliness, but denying the power thereof…" [KJV].) Honestly, I am afraid that many of the good people who have spent a lot of time in "silent worship" before God will be in for a shock when they find themselves in the presence of the heavenly hosts:

> *And I looked, and I heard the voice of many angels around the throne and the living creatures and the elders; and the number of them was myriads of myriads, and thousands of thousands,*
>
> *Saying with a loud voice, "Worthy is the Lamb that was slain to receive power and riches and wisdom and might and honor and glory and blessing."*
>
> *And every created thing which is in heaven and on the earth and under the earth and on the sea, and all things in them, I heard saying, "To Him who sits on the throne, and to the Lamb, be blessing and honor and glory and dominion forever and ever."*
>
> *And the four living creatures kept saying, "Amen." And the elders fell down and worshiped.*
>
> *And I saw when the Lamb broke one of the seven seals, and I heard one of the four living creatures saying as with a voice of thunder, "Come"* (Revelation 5:11–6:1).

I want to suggest reading many other Scriptures that further illustrate the proper balance between a godly fear of the Lord and joyful praise and intense worship. We lean too much on our "silent offerings" to the Lord. We have reviewed biblical evidence that tells us that people before the birth, death, and resurrection of Jesus Christ enjoyed a richer praise and worship life than most of us do! What does that say to you? I know what it does in my heart—something in my spirit declares: *Something is terribly wrong here! Those people didn't even have the indwelling Presence of the Holy Spirit in their lives! They didn't have the gospel of Jesus or the Book of Acts. Yet they worshiped more freely, joyfully, and powerfully than any of*

us! They saw fire and glory interrupt their services because God in-
sisted on personally taking over their worship services! Something's
broken and needs some fixin'!

The Book of Jeremiah tells us what God does when something is "broken" in His Kingdom. One day God told His
prophet to go down to the potter's house—He was going to
give the man an illustrated sermon:

> *"Arise and go down to the potter's house, and there I shall*
> *announce My words to you."*

> *Then I went down to the potter's house, and there he was,*
> *making something on the wheel.*

> *But the vessel that he was making of clay was spoiled*
> *["marred" KJV] in the hand of the potter; so he remade it*
> *into another vessel, as it pleased the potter to make.*

> *Then the word of the Lord came to me saying,*

> *"Can I not, O house of Israel, deal with you as this potter*
> *does?" declares the Lord. "Behold, like the clay in the pot-*
> *ter's hand, so are you in My hand, O house of Israel"* (Jere-
> miah 18:2-6).

Every time I think of this story of the potter's wheel, I remember that we are in God's hands. When we get "spoiled"
or marred, we usually think God has dropped us. The truth
is that we became marred in the Potter's hands because of
our own actions, our wrong choices, or just because when
crazy things happen in our lives, we temporarily have lapses
and begin to think we are lord and He is not. You don't have
to get outside of God to get your life messed up. You can be
serving Him and walking with Him daily, and yet still be
"marred" by resisting the gentle molding of His fingers in a
particular area of your life.

The fact is that He is the potter, and we are the clay. I remember the time I heard an anointed song that is based on
this passage in Jeremiah. It came at a time in my life when I

needed to hear that God could make me new again. I wanted to start all over as a new vessel, and the truth encased in song brought a new refreshing and hope to my life.

Just as God picked up the pieces of my life and revived my soul, He also can pick up your broken pieces and fix them. If you have any rivers that you think are uncrossable, I can tell you that He is the Bridge over all troubled waters. He is a tunnel through your biggest mountain!

If you want to get your car fixed, do you get a pet care manual for your dachshund to help you fix your car? No. If you have a Ford, do you get a Cadillac manual? No, you have to get the right manual from the creator of what is broken!

If some things in our local churches are broken (and they are), then we need to go back to the Author and Finisher of our faith to find wholeness. Think of the people in your local church and ask yourself: "Whose church is this?" The answer is obvious: It's the Lord's church. That means He has the exclusive right to say how He wants us to live and behave in it. One of the things that He seems to say about worship and praise in the last part of His instruction manual is that we're going to need supernatural eardrums in Heaven because it's loud up there! "After these things I looked, and behold, a door standing open in heaven, and the first voice which I had heard, like the sound of a trumpet speaking with me, said, 'Come up here...' " (Rev. 4:1).

Now if you know anything about trumpets, then you know they are loud. (If an angel walked into your worship service and blew a trumpet, would folks jump up out of their pews in joy or just fall down in stunned shock?) The trumpet sounds are just the beginning. Look at what happens next:

"Come up here, and I will show you what must take place after these things."

Immediately I was in the Spirit; and behold, a throne was standing in heaven, and One sitting on the throne...

And around the throne were twenty-four thrones; and upon the thrones I saw twenty-four elders sitting, clothed in white garments, and golden crowns on their heads.

And from the throne proceed flashes of lightning and sounds and peals of thunder (Revelation 4:1b-5a).

Thrones, flashing lightning, sounds and peals of thunder. Would you agree that these things suggest that maybe there is some noise going on in the throne room of God? The sixth verse describes four living creatures "full of eyes in front and behind" around the throne of God. These creatures may be the noisiest of them all:

And day and night they do not cease to say, "HOLY, HOLY, HOLY, is THE LORD GOD, THE ALMIGHTY, WHO WAS AND WHO IS AND WHO IS TO COME."

And when the living creatures give glory and honor and thanks to Him who sits on the throne, to Him who lives forever and ever,

The twenty-four elders will fall down before Him who sits on the throne, and will worship Him who lives forever and ever, and will cast their crowns before the throne, saying,

"Worthy art Thou, our Lord and our God, to receive glory and honor and power; for Thou didst create all things, and because of Thy will they existed, and were created" (Revelation 4:8b-11).

They keep this up day and night! They never stop saying, "Holy, holy, holy is the Lord God Almighty, who was, and is, and is to come." We all need to get in synchronization with Heaven and join in their endless song of praise and worship. Say it out loud right now: "Holy, holy, holy is the Lord God Almighty, who was, and is, and is to come!" Now say it a little louder: "Holy, holy, holy is the Lord God Almighty, who was, and is, and is to come!"

The Bible is the ultimate hymnbook if you haven't noticed. The Bible says that they sang in a *loud voice*, "Worthy is the Lamb, that was slain, to receive power and riches and wisdom and might and honor and glory and blessing" (Rev. 5:12). Many of us think it's "orderly" in Heaven. We think it's just nice, and neat, and packaged, but Heaven is not like that at all. It's loud! It's bigger than Woodstock.

If you have been telling yourself, "Oh, I just want a little cabin on a hillside over in glory land, where I can just be quiet, just me and Jesus. I want to go to a place where we can have our own thing going, where we won't need anybody else," then you're going to be disappointed. Everybody will be extroverted up there, with one focus: the Lamb. Jesus Himself, the Lamb, will be the light for that holy city.

As members in particular of the Church of Jesus Christ, we need to listen to what they're saying in Heaven right now. If our holy instruction manual tells us they're saying, "You are worthy, O Lord our God, to receive glory, honor, and power," then we need to be declaring, "You are worthy to take the scroll and open its seals." We need to shout with loud voices, "Worthy is the Lamb who was slain to receive power, and wealth, and wisdom, and strength, and honor, and praise, and glory. Worthy is the Lamb, worthy is the Lamb, worthy is the Lamb, worthy is the Lamb!"

God's Word describes worship as an action filled with power, authority, devotion, submission, anointing, and intimacy. The world pictures it as a dead, meaningless religious exercise reserved for joyless religious people. The truth is that it is a holy function enjoyed by angels, men, and the entire created universe. Yet there is a special level of worship reserved solely for those who have been redeemed by the blood of the Lamb of God. You and I need to enter into that worship with all of our hearts. It is time for us to conform to the heavenly pattern and increase the volume and intensity of our high worship to the King of Kings and Lord of Lords until He joins us in our unity!

Part II
Postures of Worship

Chapter 4

Uplifted Hands Signal Victorious Sacrifice!

O Lord, I call upon Thee; hasten to me! Give ear to my voice when I call to Thee!

May my prayer be counted as incense before Thee; the lifting up of my hands as the evening offering (Psalm 141:1-2).

The next time you feel like keeping your hands stuck in your pockets or clinging to a purse during a worship, I want you to remember Elijah the prophet. In First Kings, chapter 18, Elijah alone faced 950 prophets of Baal and the Asherah in a showdown by fire in front of the men of Israel. By midday, the idol worshipers were still carrying on.

And it came about when midday was past, that they raved until the time of the offering of the evening sacrifice; but there was no voice, no one answered, and no one paid attention.

Then Elijah said to all the people, "Come near to me." So all the people came near to him. And he repaired the altar of the Lord which had been torn down (1 Kings 18:29-30).

Elijah waited to rebuild the altar of the Lord until "the time of the evening sacrifice." It didn't matter to him that the lunatic prophets of false gods raved, waved, and cut themselves all day long in front of their deaf and dumb idols.

Elijah was expecting something to take place at the time of the evening sacrifice. He was so confident of it that he told the fickle men of Israel, "I want you to get close to me. I want you to see what's about to take place."

When we talk about the evening sacrifice, we are talking about a time when we *expect something to take place in our presence, and we expect something to take place in the heavenlies.* The bottom line is that we should expect to see *God descend in His glory* in response to our gift!

The Psalmist wrote, "May my prayer be counted as incense before Thee; the lifting up of my hands as the evening offering" (Ps. 141:2). He is really saying, "Lord, when You see my hands lifted up to You, let them represent to You the same thing that the evening sacrifice represents to You."

In Numbers, chapter 18, the Lord tells Moses something peculiar concerning the priestly tribe of Levites. Set apart to serve God in priestly worship, this tribe owned no land, operated no businesses, and farmed no land. Instead, they were supported through the tithes (10 percent) given by the other 11 tribes of Israel. God told Moses to tell the Levites:

> ...*you shall present an offering from it to the Lord, a tithe of the tithe.*
>
> *And **your offering shall be reckoned to you** as the grain from the threshing floor or the full produce from the wine vat* (Numbers 18:26b-27).

Do you understand what God is saying in verse 27? He is telling this tribe of priestly servants, "I will count your *one percent* tithe offering as if it is the *entire* grain offering from the threshing floor or all of the *full produce* taken from the winepress." Now think about King David's prayer. When David, the psalmist, prayed to God, "Let the lifting of my hands be as the evening sacrifice," he was really saying, "In Your heart and mind, God, let the offering of my lifted hands be no different from the total evening sacrifice!"

What does that mean for us? If we can overcome our awkwardness and pride enough to lift our hands in true praise and worship to God, then He will *leverage* or increase the value and impact of that worship exponentially! A lot of people come to worship, but when they see folks worshiping God without inhibitions or hangups, they ask, "Why do they have their hands lifted up anyway? What does it all mean?"

I saw a cartoon once where a guy was in a very conservative and staid church. As the minister was speaking in very somber, sober tones, this guy was sitting out in the audience. Every time the minister would say something, the guy would say "Hallelujah, amen! Yes, praise the Lord."

Finally, an usher, who was dressed in a formal outfit complete with white gloves, leaned over and said, "We don't praise the Lord in this church!" (Well, you know what he meant: "We don't praise the Lord out loud, we don't lift our hands, we don't clap; we offer silent sacrifices.")

We have already established that the ultimate worship handbook is the Bible. If we really want to know how to worship God, then we need to look in the Bible and see what the great leaders of the faith did when they worshiped God. What they did will work for us as well as it did for them because they are a lot closer to the pattern than we are. Yes, the Old Testament system of animal sacrifices has been replaced by the greater sacrifice of the Sacrificed Lamb of God, Jesus Christ. Yet the patterns of worship established by King David produced results that we just aren't seeing in our worship. That tells me we still have some things to learn and a considerable way to go!

If you don't know how to worship, you have a serious problem because you could be offering something to God that He really doesn't want! If He is asking for obedience in a problem area of your life, but all you give Him is a 10 percent tithe check every other week, then you are displeasing

God! You might think you are being holy when you are really on dangerous ground because of disobedience.

I attended a meeting about a decade ago with several thousand pastors from around the country. We were in the middle of a tremendous time of worship right after Ern Baxter had preached a message on the resurrection—a message that made us believe that Jesus could come at any moment. In fact, a lot of us were looking up at the ceiling as we fully expected Him to come at any time.

While we entered even deeper into worship, a prophetic word came forth that declared: "Take off your shoes, for the ground where you stand is holy ground."

Thousands of voices responded, "Yeah, hallelujah, amen!" But when I looked up on the platform, I noticed that a respected teacher by the name of Derek Prince had slipped his shoes off!

When I looked at him, I thought, *What's wrong with Derek? Why has he taken his shoes off?* Then it suddenly dawned on me: *Derek Prince believed the prophecy and acted accordingly.*

When God says, "Take your shoes off," you had better take those shoes off! It doesn't matter whether you have holes in your socks or not. Take them off and enjoy the fruits of obedience, because disobedience plus sacrifice still equals disobedience.

David prayed, "May my prayer be counted as incense before Thee; the lifting up of my hands as the evening offering" (Ps. 141:2). I want you to understand something about worship and what takes place when you lift up your hands to the Lord. Hosea the prophet declared:

> *Return, O Israel, to the Lord your God, for you have stumbled because of your iniquity.*
>
> ***Take words with you*** *and return to the Lord. Say to Him, "Take away all iniquity, and receive us graciously, that we may **present the fruit of our lips**"* (Hosea 14:1-2).

The King James Version of the Bible translates the last part of this passage this way: "so will we render the *calves* of our lips." In this case, the King James Version agrees with the original Hebrew manuscripts, which contain an obvious reference to the animal sacrifices made for the atonement of sin. When you offer a sacrifice, you're giving God something. But God is not merely interested in what you burn on some altar. Today He asks us to give Him the sacrifice or fruit of our lips, as we give thanks unto Him and worship Him. This is echoed and confirmed under the New Covenant in the Epistle to the Hebrews: "Through Him then, let us continually offer up a sacrifice of praise to God, that is, the fruit of lips that give thanks to His name" (Heb. 13:15). Look closely at this revolutionary Old Testament passage:

But I am afflicted and in pain; May Thy salvation, O God, set me securely on high.

*I will praise the name of God **with song**, And shall magnify Him **with thanksgiving**.*

*And **it will please the Lord better than an ox or a young bull** with horns and hoofs.*

The humble have seen it and are glad; you who seek God, let your heart revive.

For the Lord hears the needy, and does not despise His who are prisoners (Psalm 69:29-33).

When you are offering God thanksgiving, according to the Scriptures you are offering Him "a better sacrifice than a burnt bull." The praises and worship of your lips are your sacrifices, your bulls, your meal offerings, your first fruits. No, they don't replace financial giving because giving is still part of God's requirement for disciples, but the sincere words of your lips are of great value to God. The apostle Peter wrote to the churches:

And coming to Him as to a living stone, rejected by men, but choice and precious in the sight of God,

*You also, as living stones, are being built up as a spiritual house for a holy priesthood, to offer up **spiritual sacrifices** acceptable to God through Jesus Christ* (1 Peter 2:4-5).

When you enter into worship, you are offering spiritual sacrifices that are just as real to God as literal sacrifices of bullocks, oxen, heifers, rams, and goats. You also are giving meal offerings. When your prayers go up before God, they are real to God. When most people say "spiritual," they are thinking: *Spiritual—yeah, something that's not real.* The truth is that the spiritual is more real than the natural! The spiritual realm is going to last a lot longer than natural things. What does God say about the spiritual sacrifices we offer to Him? They are "acceptable" to God.

Why did David pray about the lifting of his hands? The things we do with our hands have far more meaning than most people would ever dream! Even a quick survey of the role of "hands" in the Scriptures will turn up some real surprises. The lifting of the hands is associated with the taking of an oath: "And Abram said to the king of Sodom, I have *lift up mine hand* unto the Lord, the most high God, the possessor of heaven and earth" (Gen. 14:22 KJV). Ezekiel the prophet wrote, "Thus saith the Lord God; in the day when I chose Israel, and *lifted up Mine hand* unto the seed of the house of Jacob, and made Myself known unto them in the land of Egypt, *when I lifted up Mine hand unto them,* saying, I am the Lord your God" (Ezek. 20:5 KJV).

Paul told Timothy, "Therefore I want the men in every place to pray, *lifting up holy hands,* without wrath and dissension" (1 Tim. 2:8). Sometimes when our hands are lifted up, we are saying to God, "God, I believe what I'm about to ask You to do." When Moses stood on the banks of the Red Sea with the Israelites and Pharaoh close behind, God told him:

"Why are you crying out to Me? Tell the sons of Israel to go forward.

"And as for you, lift up your staff and stretch out your hand over the sea and divide it, and the sons of Israel shall go through the midst of the sea on dry land (Exodus 14:15-16).

The upraised or stretched out hand is a biblical statement and symbol of power and divine authority. Your upraised hand speaks about what you expect God to do in response to your faith. The Psalmist wrote hundreds of years later about the day Moses extended his hand and staff over the Red Sea: "The sea looked and fled" (Ps. 114:3). Hallelujah! It is no marvel to me that the enemy doesn't want you to raise your hands.

When Moses stretched out his hands, to all appearances he was just extending a rod. But the greater reality is that he was determining the outcome of a crisis. When he held his hands up with the help of Aaron and Hur on a hilltop later on, he looked pretty silly to the natural man. But the greater reality was that he was determining the outcome of a battle in the valley below.

I think that many times Christians don't realize how much they are determining something beyond their scope of understanding through their obedience. And for me, the highest form of worship is obedience.

One time when I was in Hong Kong, I saw some people practicing "Tai Chi," an ancient oriental form of exercise based on martial arts movements performed at an extremely slow speed. When I saw those people practicing Tai Chi, it was the weirdest looking thing. But it was normal and natural to those people because they had been practicing those movements for years. Each of those movements was a martial exercise with a specific name. It didn't mean anything to me, initially, but then I remembered a conversation I'd had with Derek Prince years before.

I asked Derek about Yoga because I knew that when he became a Christian, he was delivered from a really powerful spirit of Yoga after practicing it for years. I asked him, "Do you still do the exercises?" At that time, I was using Yoga exercises as stretching routines because I was running a lot.

Derek said, "No, I don't do them anymore because nobody really knows what the body postures mean. When you're sitting in the lotus position or in the plow position (which is another characteristic term in yoga), you could be making key statements to the demonic world with your posture. So I don't do them anymore."

When I pulled those two pieces together—the Tai Chi thing and the statements Derek Prince made about the postures making statements to the spirit realm—I said, "I wonder then how much of what we do in our worship are statements to an invisible realm, statements that have awesome power? Perhaps God chooses and uses the weak thing of the lifting of hands, or the foolish thing of dancing in ways that I don't understand. For instance, when I worship the Lord, even if that act of worship might look foreign or foolish to someone else, perhaps it has accomplished something for God and for the purposes of God that I can't see. The Psalmist wrote, "Let the high praises of God be in their mouth...to bind their kings with chains, and their nobles with fetters of iron" (Ps. 149:6-8). That means my worship to God is really fulfilling a function in Heaven that is beyond my scope.

How much more often would that happen if I really understood what happens when I obediently worship God? When someone says, "Let's just lift our hands before Him," is it possible that just the simple act of lifting our hands before God enables Him to do something as powerful as He did when Joash shot the arrow out of the window toward the east? Outwardly this action appeared to be an absolutely foolish thing, but it accomplished a victory.

Sometimes, when you most need to raise your hands—when you are impressed by the Holy Spirit to raise them up—you will have something come over you that says, "I don't feel like raising my hands." Now that little voice talking to you is really the adversary. He doesn't want you to raise your hands because the moment that you do you're really saying, "*In your face, devil!*" Frankly, satan doesn't want God or God's anointed representative in his face!

In Isaiah 13:2, God's Word says, "Raise a banner on a bare hilltop, shout to them; beckon to them to enter the gates of the nobles" (NIV). In modern terms, God is saying, "Look, if you don't like what's going on in your neighborhood, go out and lift your hands up to Me before they put the gun on you!" Let the lifting of your hands be a victory flag! Let the lifting of your hands be the same thing as when Moses lifted up his rod over a battlefield and watched God's people win the battle against Amalek (see Ex. 17:10-15).

There were really two battles going on in that story. One was down on the actual battlefield, and one was up on the hilltop with Moses, Aaron, and Hur. As long as Moses' hands were raised, the people of God prevailed. When the hands dropped, so did the fortunes of Israel's army. Why? As long as Moses' hands were up, *God fought for Israel.* After the battle, Moses built an altar of remembrance to God and called it Jehovah Nissi—God is my Banner.

There are a lot of folks in ministry who don't realize that their "success" didn't come because they preach so well. It came because somewhere, somebody had his hands lifted up for them. All of those victories were won in the prayer room, not the pulpit! Battles are won wherever holy hands are lifted up to God.

The Bible also tells us we can bless God with a "wave offering" today just as Aaron did according to the Book of Leviticus. Under the New Covenant, the emphasis is on our hands and the fruit of our lips rather than on the physical parts of a sacrificed animal.

> *Then he slaughtered the ox and the ram, the sacrifice of peace offerings which was for the people; and Aaron's sons handed the blood to him and he sprinkled it around on the altar.*
>
> *As for the portions of fat from the ox and from the ram, the fat tail, and the fat covering, and the kidneys and the lobe of the liver,*
>
> *They now placed the portions of fat on the breasts; and he offered them up in smoke on the altar.*
>
> *But the breasts and the right thigh Aaron presented as a **wave offering** before the Lord, just as Moses had commanded.*
>
> *Then Aaron **lifted up his hands toward the people and blessed them**, and he stepped down after making the sin offering and the burnt offering and the peace offerings.*
>
> *And Moses and Aaron went into the tent of meeting. When they came out and blessed the people, the glory of the Lord appeared to all the people.*
>
> *Then fire came out from before the Lord and consumed the burnt offering and the portions of fat on the altar; and when all the people saw it, they shouted and fell on their faces* (Leviticus 9:18-24).

In this pre-Calvary sacrifice, Aaron held up a huge chunk of meat that he had cut from the center of an animal sacrifice and waved it before the Lord. Then he lifted his bloody hands and blessed the people. Today our sins have been washed away by the precious blood of Jesus Christ, and He ever lives to intercede for us to the Father. We can still lift our hands and bless in His name—and we no longer need to wave the breast of a sacrificed animal or a bowl of grain. We can wave an offering of adoration, praise, and worship to God the Father, and we can extend our hands and bless others in the name of Jesus with much greater power and authority!

David saw past the animal sacrifices to sacrifices of the heart and hand in Psalm 134, when he declared, "Lift up your hands to the sanctuary, and bless the Lord" (Ps. 134:2). (The word *sanctuary—qodesh* in the Hebrew—could actually be translated "the Sacred One" in this verse.)

How can we bless God? How can the lesser bless the greater? First of all, God is *blessed* by our *obedience*. When Jesus submitted Himself to be baptized in the muddy Jordan (even though He was sinless), His obedience touched the heart of God who spoke out of Heaven and declared, "This is My beloved Son, in whom I am well pleased" (Mt. 3:17).

When we lift up our hands in obedience to the Spirit's prompting, we immediately become more involved in what God wants us to do. A spiritual battle might be going on somewhere—a battle in which God wants to use us through our obedience. Or He may want to do something in our own lives.

I think a lot of battles are lost because we don't obey God. I've been in a number of meetings in which I told people, "Let's lift our hands," only to see most of them stand there and stare at me.

I could almost hear them saying to themselves, "I know you're not talking to me, preacher, because I don't lift my hands for nobody!"

I have talked to my brothers about Dad's successful miracle and healing ministry. My brother's godmother said, "I used to watch him pray, and before he would put his hands on anybody, he would lift his hands before the Lord." She added, "I have yet to see him pray for anybody that God didn't touch."

Why should we lift our hands to God? By lifting our hands we are saying, "God, I promise You that You will get all of the glory" or "God, I'm telling you, I need Your help." Sometimes our uplifted hands say, "God, this is Your victory, because You're the banner, You're the winner in all of this. I'm waving the God flag when I wave Your Name over this circumstance. I'm saying to the devil, 'In your face!' "

Every time we extend our obedience beyond our thoughts to physical action, we are moved from self-consciousness to God-consciousness. We are ready to worship.

Chapter 5

He Teaches My Hands to War

Blessed be the Lord, my rock, Who trains my hands for war, And my fingers for battle (Psalm 144:1).

There is one place in every desert where you will find life-giving refreshment, and almost continual movement, activity, and violence. I'm talking about the desert oasis, where water somehow finds its way to the surface of a sea of sand. When the Israelites crossed the Red Sea and left Pharaoh and his army to sink or swim, they soon found themselves surrounded by sandy wastes without water. This happened twice, and each time, like most humans, they fell back on their natural abilities to solve the problem and promptly began to complain. God worked a miracle through Moses despite the doubt and unbelief and supplied water from a bitter pool the first time, and from a rock the second time. Everything worked out wonderfully—or did it?

The Bible says that once the Israelites found water the second time (they were much deeper into the desert by that time), then the Amalekites found *them*! Amalekites never show up until water is around. The more you ask God to water your life, the more you should expect to see "Amalekites" popping up in your life. Amalekites want water themselves, but they don't want to dig wells. They would rather jump you and steal what you have found or labored to create. The first time these descendants of Esau show up is in Exodus 17 when they confronted Moses and the sons of Israel, asking them to reveal where God gave them water. The Bible describes the incident in the Book of Deuteronomy:

> *Remember what Amalek did to you along the way when you came out from Egypt.*
>
> *How he met you along the way and* **attacked among you all the stragglers at your rear when you were faint and weary;** *and he did not fear God* (Deuteronomy 25:17-18).

The Amalekites match the Lord's description of the thief in John 10:10a: "The thief comes only to steal, and kill, and destroy...." The existence and persistence of this desert clan of thieves and murderers in the natural is a type and shadow of the spiritual predators stalking God's people in hopes of attacking the weak, the stragglers, and the separated members along the road of destiny. They also explain why God wants to *teach our hands to war!*

The dramatic battle described in Exodus 17:8-16 was especially significant because every Israelite in the battle had been raised as a slave in captivity, forbidden to own or use any weapon. Maybe I'm reading too much into this event, but in my opinion, those Israelites should have been really grateful that God was fighting for them while Moses' hands were lifted to Heaven! (See Exodus 17:11.) They were amateurs, untried warriors in harm's way fighting to defeat more experienced adversaries, and they were using the unfamiliar weapons of their former Egyptian masters.

By the time the Israelites finally crossed the Jordan to take the Promised Land, the doubting generation born in slavery had passed away. They were replaced by their desert-born children, a generation that God had transformed into a nation of seasoned warriors. Centuries later, God would use a youthful Israelite poet and shepherd to raise up and lead the largest, most deadly standing army in Asia Minor (David and his men of renown). *Anyone who dares to claim and fulfill the promises and purposes of God must become skillful in war.*

Once you get water of the Holy Spirit in your life, you can expect the "desert-dwelling Amalekites" to show up, too. Jesus' first face-to-face encounter with the devil came immediately after the Holy Spirit descended upon Him when He was baptized in the Jordan River by John the Baptist. The Bible says *the Holy Spirit* led Him to the wilderness to be tempted and tried by the devil. It's hard to believe the Holy Ghost would do that to someone, but if He did it to Jesus to fulfill God's perfect will, then He'll do it to you too! If you are ever to possess the land for God's Kingdom, you are *destined* to face some Amalekites in battle. In the process, God will train your hands for war and your fingers for battle!

What did Moses do right after the Amalekites were defeated? He built an altar. And he called it, "The Lord is my Banner" or *Jehovah Nissi.*

When you run into resistance or suffer a surprise attack from modern Amalekites, then no matter how hostile the situation may be, just put your hands up and say, "Jehovah Nissi! The Lord is my banner!" Don't fight the battle alone—wave the banner of God and release His power into the situation with upraised hands from the high ground of faith. That means the battle below can have only one outcome.

For to this end also I wrote that I might put you to the test, whether you are obedient in all things.

But whom you forgive anything, I forgive also; for indeed what I have forgiven, if I have forgiven anything, I did it for your sakes in the presence of Christ,

*In order that **no advantage be taken of us by Satan;** for **we are not ignorant of his schemes*** (2 Corinthians 2:9-11).

The apostle Paul says something later in his letter to the Corinthians that should wake us up and open our eyes:

And no wonder, for even Satan disguises himself as an angel of light.

Therefore it is not surprising if his servants also disguise themselves as servants of righteousness; whose end shall be according to their deeds (2 Corinthians 11:14-15).

"Yeah, I met satan once, and he looked like a gargoyle." No, that probably wasn't him. He is a masquerader. Now, if you tell me you met a person who glowed in the dark and said that he would give you everything you ever wanted—then I would say you've probably met the great transformer, satan. Many of the problems in our lives and churches arise because we are ignorant of satan's schemes and we allow him to outwit us. We need to follow Jesus and stay alert to satan's scheming ways. Many Christians are unaware that God also has schemes, devices, and plans. God has a master strategy and individual battle strategies for each of us.

A lot of us just need a "perspective transplant." You've heard the complaint, "Some folks are so heavenly minded that they're no earthly good." I think that we need some heavenly minded people right now! We need some folks who think heavenly thoughts instead of earthbound fleshly thoughts. Where should you be sitting right now according to the Book of Ephesians? Paul writes, "[God has] raised us up with Him, and seated us with Him in the heavenly places, in Christ Jesus" (Eph. 2:6). What angle or perspective do you have of earthly affairs when you are seated in the heavenly places? You are looking *down* on the situations.

Remember that the enemy wants to keep your focus turned away from God's strategy for world conquest. He wants you to get focused on his diabolical strategy for world conquest so he can do you in. The solution is God Himself, who "teaches your hands to war." The U.S. Treasury Department used to train new agents how to deal with counterfeit money by focusing exclusively on "the real stuff." They never exposed them to counterfeit money. They always taught them the real stuff. "Here's the real money. This is a real dollar bill. This is a real ten. This is a real five. This is a real hundred-dollar bill." These agents-in-training would study the real thing for weeks and weeks. Then one day the instructors would slip some counterfeit money into the money stream. Suddenly, it would dawn on the trainees: "Hey, there's something wrong with this bill!"

God is trying to get us focused on the real, but the world wants us to focus on the counterfeit. "Study the cults. Study these fringe groups. Study the satanists and the New Age doctrines." You don't need to study false doctrines to know one when you hear it! (Just like you don't need to eat bad food to know good food.) If you grow up eating good food, the bad food will instantly stand out to you. When truth is the staple of your spiritual diet, anytime someone comes along with error, you won't look for someone to point the error out to you. You will be the one pointing it out.

God is saying, "I want to teach your hands to war. I want to teach you to do battle." This training is a process, a progression from small to large, from simple to advanced levels. Jeremiah 12:5 says, "If you have run with footmen and they have tired you out, then how can you compete with horses? If you fall down in a land of peace, how will you do in the thicket of the Jordan?"

If you haven't had battle experience, God is going to give you some. You either will enter a battle with battle experience or you will enter it without experience. I recommend you get the experience! God teaches your hands to war by letting you go through situations and difficulties that force you to overcome by using tools and abilities beyond your own strength and ability.

> *Now these are the nations which the Lord left, to test Israel by them (that is, all who had not experienced any of the wars of Canaan;*
>
> *Only in order that the generations of the sons of Israel might be taught war, those who had not experienced it formerly* (Judges 3:1-2).

Most of us expect to learn warfare in a classroom or Sunday school class setting with chalkboards and Bible charts. Yes, you can learn principles of warfare in the safety of your seat, but once you learn the principles, *you are accountable for their application.*

God left enemies in the land just so He could test all those Israelites who had not experienced any of the wars in Canaan. The only way to learn warfare is through tests and trials. The Hebrew word for *teach* is *lamad.* It means "to exercise in"[1] and "to goad"[2] [as if encouraging cattle to move through an unfamiliar gate or to pull a plow, using an ox goad or a "cattle prod"]. It is much stronger and more action-oriented than our static English meaning for the word *teach.* Obviously, God wants to teach His people some very specific things about warfare.

Now, we understand—and we've been ingesting this again and again and again—that the weapons of our warfare are not fleshly. They are not carnal. They are not natural weapons. But you've got to hear this. We do have warfare, and we do have weapons. We do have enemies. We do have foes. They are in the heavenlies. They are not next door to you. They are not your bosses. They are not your mates. They are not your spouses. They are not the political candidates. Somewhere we're going to have to get a drama team to do something—to act out a puppet thing where the real power is in the heavenlies and we down here will be manipulated by the powers. It can be more clearly seen.

Some people say, "Man, I don't know what's going on in my life. I don't understand what's taking place." Get in the real world. God has left some enemies here. And if you haven't had any war experience, you're going to get some. That's part of a test. It's part of a teaching. It's part of your learning experience.

God's Word carefully catalogs skills in warfare: "The sons of Reuben and the Gadites and the half-tribe of Manasseh, consisting of valiant men, men who bore shield and sword and shot with bow, and were skillful in battle, were 44,760, who went to war" (1 Chron. 5:18). In a later chapter, the Word says, "Now these are the heads of the mighty men whom David had, who gave him strong support in his kingdom, together with all Israel, *to make him king*, according to the word of the Lord concerning Israel" (1 Chron. 11:10).

What was their goal and purpose? "To make him king" (the New International Version says they "gave his kingship strong support *to extend it* over the whole land"). What should be the goal of the Church? To extend the Kingdom of Jesus Christ over the whole land! It's going to take some warfare to reach that goal. We will have to cast out demons and heal the sick. At some point, we even will have to raise the dead to get the job done.

Training makes the difference between success and failure in almost every area of life. The Bible is filled with stories of people who overcame adversity by trusting God and yielding to His training. David didn't start out on top. He didn't always have a mighty army of skilled warriors backing him up:

So David departed from there and escaped to the cave of Adullam; and when his brothers and all his father's household heard of it, they went down there to him.

And everyone who was in distress, and everyone who was in debt, and everyone who was discontented, gathered to him; and he became captain over them. Now there were about four hundred men with him (1 Samuel 22:1-2).

David *trained* his men of war the old-fashioned way—by conducting war (in his case, against the Philistines). What a motley crew. "David, I'm in debt. Will you be my pastor?" "David, I'm so upset and discontent with my church where I've been. Will you be my pastor?" These men were distressed, and David's task was to teach them to become mighty men of war. How do you do that with discontented, indebted, distressed people? You do it very lovingly, very patiently. The results of David's labors are legendary.

And these constitute the list of the mighty men whom David had: Jashobeam, the son of a Hachmonite, the chief of the thirty; **he lifted up his spear against three hundred whom he killed at one time**.

And after him was Eleazar the son of Dodo, the Ahohite, who was one of the three mighty men.

He was with David at Pasdammim when the Philistines were gathered together there to battle, and there was a plot of ground full of barley; and the people fled before the Philistines.

And they took their stand in the midst of the plot, and defended it, and **struck down the Philistines***; and the Lord saved them by a great victory* (1 Chronicles 11:11-14).

I seriously doubt that any of us will be expected to swing a sword in a physical battle on God's behalf, but we may be drafted for service as a worshiper and prayer warrior. Even in David's day, singers were considered important assets in the house of God. They too required training and skill to do their job.

All these were under the direction of their father to sing in the house of the Lord, with cymbals, harps and lyres, for the service of the house of God. Asaph, Jeduthun and Heman were under the direction of the king.

*And their number who were **trained in singing to the Lord**, with their relatives, **all who were skillful**, was 288* (1 Chronicles 25:6-7).

From the battlefield to the tabernacle of God, David trained and directed highly trained, proven men who were skilled in their particular discipline. They had won renown "by reason of use" and through hard-won experience in action. If you are going to be a warrior, you will need some experience in war. God is too wise to drop you in the middle of the hottest and most sophisticated battle when you have never been in battle before. He begins our training by overcoming small obstacles and spiritual opponents and then moves us on to larger, more formidable battles as our abilities, skills, and confidence grows.

The writer of the Epistle to the Hebrews says, "But solid food is for the mature, who because of practice have their senses trained to discern good and evil" (Heb. 5:14). Solid food is for the *mature*. Mature believers are people who have *practiced* and used their spiritual senses again and again in direct confrontation with the enemy. They aren't fooled easily. They can spot the differences between good and evil with confidence because they are *experienced*. If you are mature, you will be able to see what others can't see because you've been there before.

Near the end of his earthly life, the apostle Paul wrote, "I have fought the good fight, I have finished the course, I have kept the faith" (2 Tim. 4:7). God wants you to fight a good fight too. But you can't even make a good stand if you don't know what the fighting is all about. Hebrews 6:1 says, "Therefore leaving the elementary teaching about the

Christ, let us press on to *maturity*...." He ends his urgent appeal to the people to go on to maturity by saying, "And this we shall do, if God permits" (Heb. 6:3). Say these words with me please. "We cannot go on to maturity unless God permits us to."

Now, here's what I want to say to you. God will not permit you to go on to maturity and bypass any grade. You don't skip grades in the Kingdom. "This is first grade, son."

You may say, "Okay. What if I don't like it?"

God says, "Then you spend a lot of time here." He trains us. He teaches us. He opens our ears to listen as one being taught. One of the principle reasons that David's kingdom was extended beyond any other kingdom was: David encountered and reached more boundaries in his rule than any other. This happened because the primary aspect of David's kingdom was worship and praise.

It's phenomenal what God can do when people are praising Him. He's training my hands; He's teaching me. I'm becoming skilled in this thing. I'm learning how to say, "God, I worship You." I'm learning that the lifting of my hands is the same as a sacrifice. I'm learning that I can put a high hand in the enemy's face.

Don't despise the day of your training. Don't despise the day of small things. I honestly believe there are things that God is going to show us in the future that are the result of our obedient and *skilled* warfare in worship today! I believe He will call us and say, "Come here. Let Me show you what you were doing in 1992, and then on Christmas night in 1994, and in August of 1997. Each time you raised your hands high in the air in My name on those occasions, these key events took place in the heavenlies."

At that point, we will probably say, "Oh, Lord God, if we had only known how much *more* we could have given ourselves to worship...."

If the music David played on a single instrument literally drove evil spirits away from King Saul, then we need to wage Spirit-led warfare by worshiping God and playing on a hundred or a thousand instruments! What evil influence would be ejected from your city or this planet at that point? Can you see the picture of the hidden potential of our secret weapon of worship?

The Church is only beginning to understand the power God has planted in its people. A minister in Argentina goes to cities that historically have been closed to the gospel. Prayer teams go in two or three weeks ahead of him and lock themselves in a hotel room where they worship, pray, fast, and call out to God to reveal the principalities and the strong men in that area. Then, they decisively deal with all opposing forces in the heavenlies from the seat of the Savior's power. It is no wonder that this ministry has had remarkable revivals—their Spirit-inspired invasion strategy is just awesome! In every meeting, they see people come to the Lord as their demons come out. Multitudes are healed!

"Blessed be the Lord, my rock, who trains my hands for war, and my fingers for battle" (Ps. 144:1). My friend, you better get your fingers ready to do battle. The King is at the gate and His battle summons is ringing in your ears.

Endnotes

1. *New American Standard Exhaustive Concordance of the Bible* (The Lockman Foundation, 1981), **teach** (H3925).

2. *Strong's*, **teach** (H3925).

Chapter 6

Laying the Ambush of Worship and Praise

I was the guest minister at a church one Sunday night when I witnessed perhaps the finest thing I've ever seen in my life. I watched a man dance before the Lord during the worship service. This man was focused totally on God; he was incredibly uninhibited. Also, he was absolutely spastic—he couldn't get his rhythm together and his limbs seemed to have no coordination that I could see. It was just a hilarious sight in the natural realm, but in the spirit realm, things were altogether different. I had the impression as I watched all of this that God didn't mind in the least that this uncoordinated man was looking foolish on His behalf. The man was dancing in joy before the Lord because he loved Him.

If you have a problem with looking foolish, you just ought to go ahead, look foolish, and get it over with. Sometimes "foolishness" is the only way to accomplish the will and purpose of God.

Noah looked foolish building one of the largest wooden structures of his time while claiming it was going to float on a worldwide flood that was on its way. Abraham looked foolish when he stood over his son, Isaac, with the knife of sacrifice in his hand. Moses looked foolish sitting on a hilltop flanked by two guys holding up his arms while thousands of people fought to the death below him. Hannah looked foolish in Eli's eyes as she prayed fervently in the house of God, and David looked foolish standing in front of Goliath armed with only a leather sling and five smooth stones.

Mary looked foolish when she became pregnant as a virgin, and Joseph looked just as foolish when he agreed to marry her anyway (although he would not be intimate with his wife until after the birth of her mystery child). Meanwhile, the nosy neighbors in Judea probably counted the months backward from the birth of Jesus and came to their own conclusions. Jesus looked foolish when, as a local carpenter's son, He stood in the synagogue and read the familiar passage from the scroll of Isaiah and said, "Today this Scripture has been fulfilled in your hearing" (Lk. 4:21). His archenemy, satan, thought Jesus looked even more foolish the day that He was stretched out on a Roman cross between two crucified thieves after claiming to be the Son of God...but He wasn't foolish. He was doing the will of His Father.

Have you looked foolish for God lately? Have you dared to worship Him the way He commands us to worship in His Word? There may be much more at stake than you have ever dreamed.

And the Lord will cause His voice of authority to be heard...

For at the voice of the Lord Assyria will be terrified, when He strikes with the rod.

And every blow of the rod of punishment, which the Lord will lay on him, will be with the music of tambourines and lyres; and in battles, brandishing weapons, He will fight them (Isaiah 30:30-32).

There are certain "postures of worship" that constitute "non-verbal communication" of eternal significance under the orchestration of the Holy Spirit. In a sense, there are two forms of worship—one is the classical form we think of, which involves bowing ourselves in love and adoration before our great God. The second is more unconventional in nature—it is *obedience* in all of its varied forms. Moses was worshiping God when he obeyed and extended his hand over the Red Sea. Elijah the prophet was worshiping God when, three times, he ordered the crowd to throw more water on the wood and sacrifice stacked on the rebuilt altar of God. Look carefully at "whose word" Elijah was following:

Then it came about at the time of the offering of the evening sacrifice, that Elijah the prophet came near and said, "O Lord, the God of Abraham, Isaac and Israel, today let it be known that Thou art God in Israel, and that I am Thy servant, and that I have done all these things at Thy word.

"Answer me, O Lord, answer me, that this people may know that Thou, O Lord, art God, and that Thou hast turned their heart back again."

Then the fire of the Lord fell, and consumed the burnt offering and the wood and the stones and the dust, and licked up the water that was in the trench.

And when all the people saw it, they fell on their faces; and they said, "The Lord, He is God; the Lord, He is God" (1 Kings 18:36-39).

Samuel the prophet said it perfectly when he told Saul in First Samuel 15:22, "Has the Lord as much delight in burnt offerings and sacrifices as in obeying the voice of the Lord? Behold, to obey is better than sacrifice, and to heed than the fat of rams."

The Holy Spirit, who directs our worship, will say from time to time, "Do this" and "Do that." Sometimes, He clearly will ask or impress upon us the need to physically bow before the Lord, to kneel, to lift our hands, or to clap. Sometimes, we are exhorted to shout for joy or to dance. The fact is that many of the "foolish" or unexplained things the Spirit asks us to do in our worship and prayer times have a direct effect on both the seen and unseen realms.

In the tenth chapter of the Book of Daniel, we see where Daniel prayed, fasted, and interceded for 21 days when he sensed a supernatural "mourning" come over him. At the end of the 21-day period, an angel appeared to him and confirmed that God had heard his prayer the very *first day* Daniel went to prayer. The angel explained that he had been hindered by a powerful demonic prince or principality assigned to Persia, where Daniel lived. It was the fervent prayer of Daniel that enabled God's messenger to hold fast until the archangel Michael could come to help. Daniel's actions in Spirit-inspired prayer in a closed room in Persia affected the heavenlies where the real battle between angelic powers took place.

Paul the apostle said, "For our struggle is not against flesh and blood, but against the rulers, against the powers, against the world forces of this darkness, against the spiritual forces of wickedness in the heavenly places" (Eph. 6:12). What many Christians don't realize is that this struggle is conducted through our *worship and praise* as much as it is through our prayers and actions on earth. Look closely at the Scripture we quoted earlier in this chapter:

> *And the Lord will cause His voice of authority to be heard...*
>
> *For at the voice of the Lord Assyria will be terrified, when He strikes with the rod.*
>
> *And every blow of the rod of punishment, which the Lord will lay on him, will be with the music of tambourines and lyres; and in battles, brandishing weapons, He will fight them* (Isaiah 30:30-32).

The tambourine is a precursor of all of the modern drums that we have today. It was used to establish the rhythm and cadence of what was taking place.

Praise the Lord! Sing to the Lord a new song, and His praise in the congregation of the godly ones.

Let Israel be glad in his Maker; let the sons of Zion rejoice in their King.

Let them praise His name with dancing; let them sing praises to Him with timbrel [tambourine] and lyre [harp].

For the Lord takes pleasure in His people; He will beautify the afflicted ones with salvation.

Let the godly ones exult in glory; let them sing for joy on their beds.

Let the high praises of God be in their mouth, **and a two-edged sword in their hand,**

To execute vengeance on the nations, and punishment on the peoples;

To bind their kings with chains, and their nobles with fetters of iron;

To execute on them the judgment written; this is an honor for all His godly ones. Praise the Lord! (Psalm 149:1-9).

Read verse 6 again with me: "Let the high praises of God be in their mouth, and a two-edged sword in their hand...."

Why? "To execute vengeance on the nations, and punishment on the peoples; to bind their kings with chains, and their nobles with fetters of iron; to execute on them the judgment written" (Ps. 149:7-9).

Now, I'm not interested in binding the King of Sweden, the King of England (when they have one), or any other ruler, president, chairman, secretary, prime minister, diplomat, despot, tribal chief, or ambassador extraordinaire. Earthly kings don't hold the real power on the earth. We're after the real "power behind the thrones" and governments of the earth. God dispatched an angel to Daniel to calm his concerns over the future of Israel. That angel described in incredible detail every major political shift of power among the nations. The angel outlined the shift of world domination from the Babylonian empire to the Medo-Persian empire and then described the rise and fall of Alexander the Great (Greece), along with the ascendancy of the great Roman Empire. And behind it all were the battling principalities and powers of the heavenlies.

Don't be deceived by events taking place in your hometown, or in Washington, DC, or Rome, Jerusalem, or London. The real powers are not sitting in the houses of Congress, in the parliaments, assemblies, or even in the military headquarters of the so-called super powers. The real powers in the heavenlies manipulate these so-called earthly powers. If you don't understand this, then I can guarantee that you will be frustrated. Picket signs don't affect the real powers behind earthly powers. These principalities in the heavenlies (which are *not* necessarily the highest Heaven of God's habitation) are not intimidated when the Church has a public macramé session. I think demons pass or float by our churches and listen to see what's going on. I can imagine them saying:

"Oh, they're doing macramé in there again. Just keep right on going."

"How about that one?"

"Oh no, they're into aerobic dancing this week. Just keep right on going."

Church activities that have little or nothing to do with the realm of the spirit don't bother the demonic realm. But if you decide to have a prayer meeting, then don't be surprised if the first thing that goes is the sound system! (After all, the devil is called "the prince of the power of the air.") Nevertheless, God created us to worship Him, to praise Him, and to seek Him with all of our being. In return, He is pleased to use our obedience to literally strike death-dealing blows on our enemies in the heavenlies!

The Book of Revelation tells us that an angel will bind satan with a "great chain" for a thousand years (see Rev. 20:1-2). Most of us realize this is apocalyptic imagery, or natural word pictures used to describe a supernatural reality. God wants us to understand that He's talking about spiritual chains that we can use against the dark kingdom when we move in the dimension of praise and anointed worship!

When we cooperate with the Holy Spirit—sing, praise, and worship God according to His instructions—He can whip a chain around one demonic power, slap something around another one, and slash another one with the flaming sword of His energized Word. It happens every time God takes delight in His people. You and I have been given the authority to bind whatever tries to get between us and the Lord. We can do it through the power of God's Word and through worship of His name.

We know the Bible says that the Lord "will cause His voice of authority to be heard" (Is. 30:30a). The New International Version says, "The Lord will cause men to hear His majestic voice." How will He do it? We know the verse is filled with imagery to portray the real thing, but what is it? The New Testament record spells it out in detail:

*But thanks be to God, who always leads us in His triumph in Christ, and manifests **through us** the sweet aroma of the knowledge of Him in every place.*

For we are a fragrance of Christ to God among those who are being saved and among those who are perishing (2 Corinthians 2:14-15).

And to bring to light what is the administration of the mystery which for ages has been hidden in God, who created all things;

*In order that the manifold wisdom of God might now be made known **through the church** to the rulers and the authorities in the heavenly places* (Ephesians 3:9-10).

We've been waiting for God to speak out of the heavens with a booming voice that will cause gridlock and upheaval in every major city across the world. But while we're down here saying, "Speak to us, Lord," He is saying, "Why don't you read My book? I want to speak through you individually and together as My Church!"

A lot of us are frustrated because the truth hasn't sunk in that the problem is not people or institutions on earth. The problem is not the gangs; it is the principality that is manipulating the gangs! That means the solution isn't in any particular program or outreach to gangs—it lies in the heavenlies. If we don't address that spiritual problem with a spiritual solution, then we can expect to have gangs proliferate like roaches.

When I was growing up, my family lived in an apartment building with three separate apartments on each side of the building. We discovered very early that all of the neighbors had to agree about their "roach policy." If one family decided to go after the roaches, then everybody had to go after roaches. I remember that one day when my mama wasn't home, we saw a bunch of roaches. Being the great hunters we were, the Garlington boys got out their guns (a can of roach spray). We started socking it to those roaches, and we were pretty proud of ourselves because those bugs just disappeared. All of a sudden, the people who lived in the apartment above us called down, "Now you all stop that down there!" We hadn't eliminated our roach problem—we had just "loaned" it to our neighbors without their permission. Those roaches ruled our roost as long as there was no consensus or unity among the residents of that apartment building about declaring war on our unwanted pests. Whether the infestation involves a natural army of insects or a supernatural crew of devils, there must be unity, determination, and the authority of the King to win the battle.

The King's authority is represented in almost every culture by a rod or scepter of authority. This is true whether you look at the older monarchies of Europe, present-day monarchies in England and Sweden, or in the African monarchies in existence today. God's Word says, "The voice of the Lord will shatter Assyria; with His scepter He will strike them down" (Is. 30:31 NIV). The Lord has delegated His name and authority to us, but we can't use God's scepter simply to do what we want. God's scepter is designed to be used for what He wants it to be used for, and He will allow no one to misuse His authority. Look at what happens when the King's authority is used correctly: "And every blow of the rod of punishment, which the Lord will lay on him, will be with the music of tambourines and lyres; and in battles, brandishing weapons, He will fight them" (Is. 30:32).

Combine this picture with the verse that tells us, "[He] trains my hands for war, and my fingers for battle" (Ps. 144:1). You are beginning to glimpse the incredible importance of Spirit-led worship and praise in the Kingdom. I can see God destroying His enemies to the beat and music of tambourines and harps.

Did you ever think that while you are worshiping down here and celebrating with joy and hilarity, God is having the same kind of fun in Heaven? Do you realize that He uses your praise and worship as weapons? I can almost imagine Him saying, "I can use that one—that's a high praise. Throw Me a higher one! I want to hit this one out of the universe."

Music has three components: melody, rhythm, harmony. The secular world understands the power of rhythm and melody. If you don't think so, then you need to listen to some of the songs being played on top secular radio stations, particularly those with a rock music format. One song recorded by the British rock group Queen has so powerfully affected large crowds that it has become "the song" at major sports events. The chorus features the words, "We will, we will rock you!" matched to a heart-throbbing beat. When that song is sung by 40,000 fans in unison with their feet stomping in time to the beat, every molecule in the sports stadium is moved with it. If you have experienced it, you won't have any trouble believing every detail of the Jericho "conquest by sound" in Joshua chapter 6.

In the hands of God, any form of worship or praise becomes lethal to the purposes of satan. At Jericho, God used the sounds of trumpets and a single great shout from His people to reconfigure the molecular makeup of Jericho's massive walls and totally collapse them to the ground so that every Israelite soldier was able to walk straight into that fortified city.

Then God sent Jehoshaphat against the enemy armed only with this song: "For the Lord is good and His mercy endureth forever." You may be thinking, "But Brother Garlington, that doesn't sound very 'warlike' to me! What kind of fear does that create?" The power isn't resident in the song—it is in the arm and hand of the One who wields it as a sword! That passage can be sung to almost any kind of rhythm, but if it comes from the heart, God can use it to destroy your enemies in the heavenlies. The point is that as we worship God in obedience to His Spirit, He says, "And every blow of the rod of punishment...will be with the music of tambourines and lyres; and in battles, brandishing weapons, [I] will fight them" (Is. 30:32).

God likes doing things to music! God asked Job who laid the earth's cornerstone, "when the morning stars sang together, and all the sons of God shouted for joy" (Job 38:7). God obviously is describing creation in this passage. What did He say was going on while He was creating? The angels (or sons of God) were *singing* and *shouting* with great joy. Can you just imagine God saying to the angelic choir, "Go ahead. Sing and shout some more. I want to get creative!"

God loves music because God Himself *is music*! God understands all of the dynamics and intricacies of music because He created it. Satan or lucifer understands music because, according to Ezekiel the prophet, he was once "the anointed cherub who covers" (Ezek. 28:14). Satan's whole framework was music. The Scriptures even describe his body as an instrument in Ezekiel 28! Now, if anyone has misused music, the enemy has. I have news for you. God is restoring all things, and He is telling the Church: *Let's get this thing straight. Music, the very gift that satan wants to use to distort truth and send people off in different directions, I will use to destroy his works in the earth.*

According to Isaiah 30:32, every time you sing and worship, God is going to use your music of worship to strike down His enemies in the earth! He will joyfully strike the Assyrian with His rod of power to the accompaniment of tambourines and harps. I can almost see the devil's imps cowering under a crippling barrage of blows on the strongholds of darkness as they hiss, "Look, if those people don't ever sing again, it would be too soon for me!" We can't overestimate the power and impact our spiritual songs, singing, and spiritual melodies have on the powers of darkness! Pray this prayer with me if you are serious about conducting warfare through praise and worship:

> *Lord, you rule in the heavenlies and You're teaching us how to rule with You. We've made it complicated. We've made it complex, and yet Your Word says, "Let the lifting of our hands be to You the same thing that the burnt offering was." Oh God, let the beating of the tambourines and the rhythmic flow of the music, the worship, and the song be to You the binding power over the enemy in the heavenlies.*

The Scriptures clearly indicate that there are hierarchical layers of spirit beings in the heavens. The Bible refers to Michael as an archangel in Jude 1:9, and the Old Testament describes cherubim, seraphim, and "winged creatures" in Heaven. It is the apostle Paul who gives us the best picture of the organization of the hosts of Heaven in Ephesians 6:12: "For our struggle is not against flesh and blood, but against the rulers, against the powers, against the world forces of this darkness, against the spiritual forces of wickedness in the heavenly places." Now that is where the battle is.

Now, if we keep that in mind, we will begin to understand that on earth there is a struggle going on that reflects the struggle going on in the heavenlies. It is God who trains our fingers for battle against the enemy. Several years ago, this prophetic word came to a church:

> *The people say it's just a simple song. God says our song is a symphony of praise unto Him and a dirge of destruction to the enemy. The people say it's just the clapping of hands, but God says in the heavenly realm it's not just a clap, but a thunderclap bringing fear to the enemy. The people say stomping the feet is just a silly thing, but God says that the stomping of feet shakes the foundations of hell creating fissures or large cracks in it. The people say the waving of flags is just a silly thing, but God says the waving of flags is a signal to the enemy of His imminent defeat and a wave offering unto God.*

When we sing, praise, and worship God together, something takes place in the spiritual dimension that we can't see. I believe that God is giving us some pictures or snapshots of what takes place in the spiritual dimension in Isaiah 30.

In 1985, our church received this prophetic word: "Know that I'm moving in a new dimension of praise. Understand that as you clap your hands you are not only praising Me,

[but] you are saying to the adversary, even as a mother would say to a cat under the table, 'Be gone, in the name of Jesus.' " It is interesting to see how this meshes so closely with the words of Isaiah: "And every blow of the rod of punishment, which the Lord will lay on him, will be with the music of tambourines and lyres" (Is. 30:32a).

God wants us to understand that our singing is not "just singing." Our worship is not just worship. We are not out to stroke an infinite ego—we are fulfilling God's purpose in the earth! As we noted earlier, God's Word declares:

> Let the **high praises of God** be in their mouth, and a two-edged sword in their hand,
>
> To execute vengeance on the nations, and punishment on the peoples;
>
> To bind their kings with chains, and their nobles with fetters of iron;
>
> To execute on them the judgment written; this is an honor for all His godly ones. Praise the Lord! (Psalm 149:6-9).

The Assyrians were a problem, but the real leader of the Assyrians wasn't on earth. He could only be found in the heavenlies with the other principalities of darkness. The true leader of Persia wasn't dwelling on the earth where Daniel was. The true king or prince of Persia ruled or dominated the earthly king from the heavenlies. God says that He will use our praises to bind their kings with fetters, their nobles with shackles of iron, and to carry out the sentence written against them. This is the glory of all His saints. It is the *glory* of the saints to carry out the sentence, according to God's Word.

A slaughter needs to take place in the heavenlies! When Babylon came down, it was because the principality of Babylon came down. When the empire of the Medo-Persians came down, it was because the principality of the Medo-Persians came down. When the Grecian kingdom came down, it was because the Grecian principality came down. I can tell you that the principalities ruling and manipulating the minds of people in your city or region only will come down when the people of God stand together and wage war with the spiritual weapons of prayer, praise, and worship. We've got to say, "If this clapping means anything at all, I'm going to get serious about it. If this lifting of the hands means anything at all, I'm going to get serious about it. And even though I look like the biggest of fools, I would rather look like a fool and accomplish something for You, Lord, than be cool and get nothing done."

One of the most exciting Bible passages for believers engaged in spiritual warfare appears in a relatively obscure passage in the Book of Second Chronicles where a prophet named Jahaziel said: "Listen, all Judah and the inhabitants of Jerusalem and King Jehoshaphat: thus says the Lord to you, 'Do not fear or be dismayed because of this great multitude, for the battle is not yours but God's' " (2 Chron. 20:15).

The punchline you need to see today is in verse 22: "And when they began *singing and praising, the Lord set ambushes* against the sons of Ammon, Moab, and Mount Seir, who had come against Judah; so they were routed." Did you see that? Let me repeat it just to make sure: "And when they began singing and praising, *the Lord set ambushes*" (2 Chron. 20:22a).

Who set the ambushes? The Lord Himself! When did He set the ambushes? *When His people began singing and praising Him!* Now answer this question: "What were they saying?" The answer is in the last half of verse 21: "And when he had consulted with the people, he appointed those who sang to the Lord and those who praised Him in holy attire, as they went out before the army and said, 'Give thanks to the Lord, for His lovingkindness is everlasting' " (2 Chron. 20:21).

Isn't it about time for all of us called by His name to set some lethal ambushes for satan's motley crew? Haven't you had enough of satan's grief and harassment? Then it is time to stop complaining and start praising and worshiping our Mighty God! His "gun" was loaded an eternity ago. His armies are waiting patiently for the sound of the trumpet and the melodies of our high praises to God. He is ready to fight our battles today on our behalf, but we need to do our part.

Part III

Heavenly Patterns

Chapter 7

Worshipers Make War in Heaven and Earth

For the weapons of our warfare are not of the flesh, but divinely powerful for the destruction of fortresses (2 Corinthians 10:4).

Anything God accomplishes in the earth is done through spiritual means using spiritual people. Yet, the Lord often requires spiritual people to do "natural" things that directly affect the supernatural. Let me rattle your cage with a series of statements:

1. The giving of tithes, offerings, and gifts are acts of war.

2. Praising God is an act of war.

3. Worshiping God is an act of war.

4. Prayer is an act of war.

5. Fasting is an act of war.

If you decide that you are going to tithe, I can almost guarantee that you suddenly will run into all kinds of opposition and "financial problems" calling for your money the following week. If you decide you are going to fast before the Lord, expect temptation. You can go to work six days a week for six months and never have anyone in the office or workplace offer you anything to eat. But if you tell your spouse tomorrow morning, "I'm not going to eat breakfast or lunch today, honey. I'm just going to fast," then 10 or 15 of your coworkers will get a "bright idea" that morning. That's the day that every one of them will bring freshly baked date-nut bread, banana bread, chocolate cookies, cake, homemade pie, and your favorite brand of ice cream to your desk!

"Don't you want some of these?" they will say.

Of course, you will try to be casual because you know from the Bible that you shouldn't broadcast the fact that you are fasting, so you say, "No, thank you."

They shake their heads in unbelief and say, "Oh come on, I've never brought you anything before."

When you say, "Well, okay" (secretly planning to take it home to eat later), your newfound benefactors will say, "Go ahead and taste it—it's the best thing I've ever made." (The unspoken threat is: "If you don't taste it, I'll be eternally offended, you ungrateful thing, you.")

Why did they have to bring all that great food on *that day*? Why didn't they bring it the day you missed breakfast and felt famished? That was the day they were eating Big Macs and hoagies and everything else, with grease dripping off the side of their mouths, but they never offered you anything. Fasting is warfare.

We are dealing with spiritual problems in this life, and it's important for us to hear that. Spiritual problems require spiritual solutions. Let me say it again: Spiritual problems require spiritual solutions. Now that we have that fixed in our minds, I need to add: Spiritual problems and solutions don't always appear to be spiritual. In fact, they sometimes look or sound absolutely foolish.

When we first looked at Psalm 144:1-2, which says the Lord "...trains my hands for war, and my fingers for battle," what were your first thoughts? It is logical to think, "Well, that's a great statement for the days when wars were fought with sword and buckler, but a few years have passed since then." No, God's Word still applies to life today. He is still training our hands for war and our fingers for battle!

There was a prophetic word given to a friend's church family in Florida that applies to every one of us. One of the key parts of the prophecy said this:

The people say it's just the clapping of hands, but God says in the heavenly realm it's not just a clap, but a thunderclap bringing fear to the enemy. The people say stomping the feet is just a silly thing, but God says the stomping of feet shakes the foundations of hell, creating fissures or large cracks in it.

What does God train our hands for? War. Our fingers? For battle. This is more than another example of Old Testament imagery. This is a classic example of seemingly "foolish" natural actions bearing powerful spiritual fruit! Psalm 47:1 says, "O Clap your hands, all peoples; shout to God with the voice of joy." Now if the President of the United States walked into the room, we would not only clap, but we also would stand in honor of his office—even if we didn't like his politics or his lifestyle. If Jesus, the Lover of our souls, walked in, wouldn't clapping be an exciting way to receive Him, too? We would give Him a standing ovation that would never end! According to God's Word, the Lord Jesus *is* in our midst whenever and wherever two or more gather together in His name (see Mt. 18:20). That means we need to clap when we gather in His name!

I've never found a Bible translation of Psalm 47:1 that says, "Clap your hands, all you Charismatics," or "Clap your

hands all you Pentecostals," or even "Clap your hands all you
Southern Baptists and Presbyterians." It says "clap your
hands all you nations" because that's what God wants it to
say. The late Corrie ten Boom used to say, "There are no
suggestions in Scripture, only commandments." When God
says to clap your hands, you need to clap your hands! He
also commands all of us to shout to Him with a voice of joy.
We need to get busy.

The Hebrew word for clapping in Psalm 47 and Nahum 3
is the word *tata.* It means to "blow, to clap, to strike, to
thrust, to drive, to give a blast." It's an explosive word. It's an
expulsive word. It's a hit word.

> *Your shepherds are sleeping, O king of Assyria; your nobles
> are lying down. Your people are scattered on the mountains,
> and there is no one to regather them.*
>
> *There is no relief for your breakdown, your wound is incur-
> able. **All who hear about you will clap their hands over
> you,** for on whom has not your evil passed continually? (Na-
> hum 3:18-19).*

Too many times, when we read in the Bible about a King
of Assyria, immediately we think of an earthly king. The text
says, "your shepherds." Now in the Old Testament, the shepherds were the kings. Assyria was an empire that had dominated civilizations in that part of the world for a number of
years. The Bible calls Jesus Christ "the King of kings and
Lord of lords" (1 Tim. 6:15; Rev. 19:16). When the Scriptures talk about Jesus being the King of Kings, the issue is
not whether or not He is King over the king of Arabia, the
king of Sweden, the ancient kings and queens of Assyria,
or the queen of Egypt. He is the King of all those who hold
sway in spiritual kingdoms. He says to this king of Assyria,
"There is no relief for your breakdown, your wound is in-
curable. *All who hear about you will clap their hands over you*"
(Nahum 3:19a).

Along with the command to clap our hands and shout to God with joy, God's Word tells us, "Let the godly ones exult in glory, let them *sing for joy* on their beds" (Ps. 149:5). When you wake up tomorrow morning, the first thing you need to do is sing a song of joy that God has put in your heart. This "praise business" is not something done exclusively in a church service or large-group setting. You can praise God anywhere!

I appeared on the Trinity Broadcasting Network with my friend, Pastor Kim Clement. He quoted from Psalm 22, which says, "Yet Thou art holy, O Thou who art enthroned upon the praises of Israel" (Ps. 22:3). Pastor Clement added, "In the Japanese translation, they take that same verse and say, 'When we praise God we build a big chair for God to come and sit in.' " The more you want God in your circumstances, the bigger you need to make the chair! Have you used your praises to make Him a little three-legged stool or a King's throne?

It is time for us to start praising God regardless of our circumstances. If we do, we will discover the truth in the verse that says, "In Thy presence is fulness of joy; in Thy right hand there are pleasures forever" (Ps. 16:11b). Use the power of praise to take dominion over the circumstances where you are. Use the difficulty of hard circumstances to sit on the throne with Jesus Christ. Look again at the psalmist's powerful picture of the saints from God's point of view:

Let the high praises of God be in their mouth, and a two-edged sword in their hand,

To execute vengeance on the nations, and punishment on the peoples;

To bind their kings with chains, and their nobles with fetters of iron;

To execute on them the judgment written; this is an honor for all His godly ones. Praise the Lord! (Psalm 149:6-9).

Do you believe this verse? Will you accept the fact that God says your job is to inflict vengeance on the nations and punishment on the peoples, to bind their kings with fetters and their nobles with shackles of iron? He says that you are to carry out the sentence written against them because it is the glory of all His saints. You are fulfilling this Scripture every time you stamp your feet to music of praise, when you play a tambourine or violin, when you play the drums or the high-sounding cymbals, when you play the organ or sing with joy to Him.

Your glory is to praise God; your glory is to rejoice in Him. When you do these things, according to God's Word, you are binding the ruling nobles (principalities and powers in the heavenlies) with chains and fetters! Listen: If you don't like what the enemy is doing in your life, then tie him up!

Remember the apostle Paul's statement in his second Epistle to the Corinthians, "For the weapons of our warfare are not of the flesh, but divinely powerful for the destruction of fortresses" (2 Cor. 10:4). God has given you spiritual weapons that will tie the hands of the spirit powers behind your enemies and circumstances. The battle is not down here. We do not wrestle against flesh and blood but against principalities, powers, the rulers of the darkness of this world, spiritual wickedness in the heavenlies (see Eph. 6:12). The battle is not at the office or in the house with your kids. The battle is not in the high school or in the abortion clinic. The battle is in the heavenlies.

If you fight *from the heavenlies*, you can subdue things in both the heavenlies and on earth even though you live in this earthly dimension! If this sounds too fantastic to believe, then look at the words of Jesus: "Truly I say to you, whatever you shall bind on earth shall be bound in heaven; and whatever you loose on earth shall be loosed in heaven" (Mt. 18:18). The language in the original Greek manuscripts is very important here. It should be translated this way for the most accurate understanding: "Whatever you bind on earth *must have already been bound* in Heaven."

If you try to bind things in your life or city—things that haven't been bound in the heavens—then you can forget it. Don't try to deal with a principality here if you haven't dealt with it in the heavenlies. Why? Jesus said, "...Or how can anyone enter the strong man's house and carry off his property, unless he first binds the strong man?" (Mt. 12:29a) Jesus was talking about casting out demons in this passage, so this applies directly to any battle involving evil forces in the heavenlies. You can't spoil an evil strongman's stuff until you tie up the strongman in the heavenlies.

Once in a while God reveals to us how He thinks. One of these places is in the Book of First Corinthians:

Because the foolishness of God is wiser than men, and the weakness of God is stronger than men.

For consider your calling, brethren, that there were not many wise according to the flesh, not many mighty, not many noble;

But God has chosen the foolish things of the world to shame the wise, and God has chosen the weak things of the world to shame the things which are strong,

And the base things of the world and the despised, God has chosen, the things that are not, that He might nullify the things that are,

That no man should boast before God (1 Corinthians 1:25-27, 29).

It is just like God to use mere human beings to fight cosmic battles against the devil's principalities and powers in the heavenlies. On top of everything else, the Lord insists on making us fight with the seemingly passive postures of worship and praise! Before we ever see 100,000 people gather and 50,000 come forward after an altar call by the man of

God, the Lord may require us to battle for those souls on our knees and through our praise and worship in the wee hours of the morning, in our prayer closets, and in small groups devoting ourselves to hours and days of intercessory prayer. Our battle weapons consist of an odd collection of tears, shouts of joy, prayers on bended knee, the clapping of our hands, and joyful dancing before His face.

Time and again—even in the Old Testament—God used people who didn't even have a sword or spear in their hands to defeat massive armies in full battle array. Unfortunately, we also see where men have failed to trust or obey God fully and received only partial results from God's miraculous provision instead of the total victory He intended for them. The flawed obedience of King Joash is especially disturbing for us, because we could easily sin in the same exact way he did! Like King Joash, we have been promised total victory over the works of the enemy, but *obedience is required.*

King Joash had a big problem in Second Kings 13:14. Israel's greatest enemy, the bully of the Middle East neighborhood in those days, had shown up at the door to deliver another beating. By this time, Israel's aged prophet was at death's door and things looked pretty grim, and the fact that King Joash hadn't been diligent in the things of God didn't help the situation. When he showed up at Elisha's bedside to beg for help, the old prophet gave him some odd instructions.

And Elisha said to him, "Take a bow and arrows." So he took a bow and arrows.

Then he said to the king of Israel, "Put your hand on the bow." And he put his hand on it, then Elisha laid his hands on the king's hands.

And he said, "Open the window toward the east," and he opened it. Then Elisha said, "Shoot!" And he shot. And he said, "The Lord's arrow of victory, even the arrow of victory over Aram; for you shall defeat the Arameans at Aphek until you have destroyed them" (2 Kings 13:15-17).

In our Western thinking mode, we would say, "Hey look, all the guy did was shoot an arrow out of a window. Big deal. I don't understand how Elisha can say that because he shot the arrow he's going to defeat the Syrians. *It's only an arrow.*" Correction: It's "only an arrow" when you have it. When God tells you to do something with an arrow, it becomes the phenomenal arrow of God. That arrow doesn't just fly out of the east window—it flies out into the eastern atmosphere of the heavenlies and invades the spiritual dimension with God's power. It inflicts lethal damage where the real rule is taking place. It brings down powers and principalities. That is why the prophet could say, "When you shot that arrow, God gave you the victory over your enemies." God loves to confound the mighty with foolish things. Look closely at the next two verses and learn a crucial lesson for your own life:

Then he said, "Take the arrows," and he took them. And he said to the king of Israel, "Strike the ground," and he struck it three times and stopped.

So the man of God was angry with him and said, "You should have struck five or six times, then you would have struck Aram until you would have destroyed it. But now you shall strike Aram only three times" (2 Kings 13:18-19).

Joash suffered from a problem that many Christians have in our day—he didn't really think the things that he did in the natural dimension were that important to the spiritual dimension. If the prophet had said, "God says clap your hands," like many believers today, he would have grudgingly clapped his hands while muttering to himself, "Okay, I'll do it as a token of obedience. Let's just humor the man of God. Like I always say, 'too spiritually minded to be any earthly good'."

Joash should have been paying closer attention during the window incident. This man was in an atmosphere where a single arrow shot from a window was wiping out his bitter enemies! He had just heard Elisha say, "...you shall defeat the Arameans [Syrians] at Aphek *until you have destroyed* them" (2 Kings 13:17). The prophet was speaking in plain-Jane, blunt, in-your-face Hebrew. The Hebrew word for *destroyed* is *kalah,* and according to the "J. Garlington Lexicon of Hebrew Street Terms," it means that you've "completely, totally, absolutely, beyond-a-doubt, annihilated and creamed" somebody.[1] When Elisha said that, he set the stage for what King Joash *should have done* next. Unfortunately, the king's doubt got in the way.

Our problem in spiritual warfare is that we think we only can give God so much. We need to err on the positive side of faith and trust! When God hands us an arrow, a song of praise, a tambourine, or a heavenly vision, we need to "beat on the ground" with it until God comes over, shakes us back to our senses, and says, "Okay already, you can quit. You can quit!" There needs to be something violent in us that will explode in obedience at the slightest word from the Lord of Lords. You and I need to believe that every word from the mouth of God is true and put our lives on the line for it.

Anything that God touches is supernatural and powerful—including you! God is calling each of us to *pull down strongholds through obedience*! When you respond to God's Word, clap to God, and shout to Him with a voice of joy, you are doing something that is special to God and lethal to the devil's bunch in the heavenlies. It can't be done any other way! It's not complicated and that is why we resist it. God isn't interested in explaining to us the trajectory of the arrow in terms of quantum physics—He isn't about to lay out the "equation" of His heavenly methodology, like Einstein's theory of relativity. No, He isn't looking for some puffed up intellectual adherents to His philosophy—He demands obedience and childlike faith from His children. God just says, "Take these arrows and beat on the ground" because

He knows we probably can handle that without hurting ourselves or anyone else in the process.

We constantly are struggling and failing because we are busy trying to achieve victory down on the earthly realm before we win it in the spirit realm. Have you ever noticed that even Jesus followed the pattern of winning in the heavenly realm first before He battled in the earthly realm? Jesus spent entire nights or the early part of each day in prayer to the Father before He ventured out to work miracles among men and destroy the earthly works of the devil. The most important key of all was that He only did what He saw His Father doing (see Jn. 5:19). That's why He thought nothing of doing "silly things" like making mud patties to heal a man's eyes or feeding thousands with a little boy's lunch. He saw it and He did it in total faith.

God wants us to learn how to move in the simplicity of worship. He is training our hands for battle and our fingers for war. Let the lifting of our hands be as the evening sacrifice! Oh, clap your hands all you people! When you raise your voice, you are smiting the enemy *with God's voice*! When you beat the tambourine, you are beating the enemy's back through God's arm as you give Him a steady beat for war. God is saying, "I want a ¾ time here, okay. Now let's go a little faster because I'm winding this one up."

You may be thinking: *Now that just sounds so far out, Brother Garlington.* That's exactly where the heavens are—far out there. What if God just tells you to dance in the middle of a worship service this week? Will you say, "God, I'm so embarrassed"?

He will just tell you, "Well, go ahead and dance anyway! Get in the spirit and let the simple things of God touch you at the very core of your experience."

These things will enable you to say, "God, teach my hands to war; teach my fingers to do battle." When God tells you to clap your hands, you need to say: "How many times, Lord?"

I can't help but wonder what would happen if the entire Church—the whole Church—including every born-again, blood-washed Baptist, Methodist, Lutheran, Pentecostal, Charismatic, transdenominational, transcontinental, non-denominational, Eastern Orthodox, Syrian and Serbian Orthodox, Armenian Catholic, Episcopalian, Orthodox Episcopalian, Church of God in Christ member, and true believers of every other type and stripe would gather together to celebrate the Lordship of Jesus Christ. What if we actually appointed a day and declared: "We are going to clap to God and shout to Him with a voice of joy for five minutes"? (I pray that we find out, and soon!)

In Matthew 18, Jesus said, "If two or three of you ever get together, I'll come and see it Myself" (see Mt. 18:20). Of course, I know the King James Version of this verse actually says, "For where two or three are gathered together in My name, there am I in the midst of them," but the original Greek favors my paraphrased version!

We need to take this authority and humble obedience right into our homes, too. Begin to think of your house and home as a battlefield where you can do battle for God. If you are embarrassed, then wait until your spouse and kids are out of the house. Lock the doors and engage the second lock so they can't get in even if they slip back early. Then practice marching around your house. March into every room and sing: "Give thanks to the Lord for His love endures forever!" If you have a business—or if you work for someone else at a place of business and you experience opposition there—you need to know that the battle has a spiritual point of origin unless you are in sin yourself. Ask if you can work overtime, or ask if you can just work late or come in early. Then, before anybody else gets there (and before you clock in), walk around the office declaring: "Give thanks to the Lord for His love endures forever!" You will be conducting covert spiritual warfare of the first order.

God takes great delight in using the simple things to confound those things that are profound. He takes great delight in using meek things to tear down mighty things. He says that every time you clap your hands He will lay a stroke on your enemy. (If you really knew and believed that God was laying a stroke on your enemy every time you clapped your hands, I believe you would clap until your hands were black and blue!) Well? What are you waiting for?

Endnote

1. Drawn from word studies in *Strong's Exhaustive Concordance*, **destroyed** or **consumed** (H3615); and *Theological Wordbook of the Old Testament*, R. Laird Harris, Gleason L. Archer, Jr., Bruce K. Waltke, eds. (Chicago: Moody Press, 1980), pp. 439-440, 982.

Chapter 8

Worship: The Pattern of Things in Heaven

Can you imagine trying to explain to someone who had tasted strawberries, but had never seen or tasted a raspberry, what raspberries are like? "Well, raspberries taste *something* like strawberries, but then they don't." Sometimes, we enter into new and exciting levels of worship and are tempted to think we "have arrived." What we don't understand is that even though New Testament worship is more mature and closer to "the perfect pattern" than Old Testament worship, it's still not heavenly worship. God is taking us somewhere that we have never been before.

You may think that I'm a little strange, but I think that if God gave us heavenly worship right now, we would explode! Does that make sense to you? I believe we couldn't handle *heavenly worship* because we don't have *heavenly bodies* yet. The Bible says, "For our conversation is in heaven; from whence also we look for the Savior, the Lord Jesus Christ: who shall change our vile body, that it may be fashioned like unto His glorious body, according to the working whereby He is able even to subdue all things unto Himself" (Phil. 3:20-21 KJV). Don't worry. This doesn't mean that we can't move higher in worship and praise right now! We have to because we have a world to win in battle through Christ.

We need to understand that we live and move in the midst of a dynamic tension between the seen and the unseen, the temporal and the eternal, the earthly and the heavenly. Throughout Scripture you will find comparisons and transitions. On the one hand, there is Moses' tabernacle of the wilderness era. Then, there is David's tabernacle, which made God's presence accessible to the common man for the first time in human history since before Adam's fall into sin. After David, things seemed to take a step backward toward the "boxing-in" of God and the separation of man from Jehovah. Yet, even David's tabernacle of intimate worship falls short of the *true tabernacle*, which God Himself pitched without the hands or plan of man.

Even under the New Covenant of the blood of Jesus Christ, we still come to worship laden with our human limitations and imperfections. It's true that we no longer face the problems common to the Old Covenant, when each worshiper had to bring a lamb, a goat, or a meal offering. We don't need to bring the blood of animals anymore. Instead, we bring the sacrifices of praise! The prophet Hosea (yes, an Old Testament prophet) says: "We offer Him the calves of our lips, the sacrifices of our lips."

Early in this book, I mentioned the revelation Jesus gave us at the well in Samaria when He told a fallen but spiritually hungry woman, "But an hour is coming, and now is, when the *true worshipers* shall worship the Father in spirit and truth; for *such people* the Father seeks to be His worshipers" (Jn. 4:23).

Now I want you to plug this elect group of *true worshipers* into "the Lord's prayer" where Jesus gave the disciples an example of God-pleasing prayer:

Pray, then, in this way: "Our Father who art in heaven, Hallowed be Thy name.

"Thy kingdom come. Thy will be done, On earth as it is in heaven" (Matthew 6:9-10).

Could it be that God wants true worshipers (you and me) to bring His rule down to the earth through the blood of the Lamb and the power of prayer, praise, worship, and obedience? I think so. We need to delve more deeply into the vital relationship between heavenly things and earthly things, which means we need to go to the Book of Hebrews.

Now the main point in what has been said is this: we have such a high priest, who has taken His seat at the right hand of the throne of the Majesty in the heavens,

A minister in the sanctuary, and in the true tabernacle, which the Lord pitched, not man.

For every high priest is appointed to offer both gifts and sacrifices; hence it is necessary that this high priest also have something to offer.

Now if He were on earth, He would not be a priest at all, since there are those who offer the gifts according to the Law;

Who serve a copy and shadow of the heavenly things, just as Moses was warned by God when he was about to erect the tabernacle; for, "SEE," He says, "THAT YOU MAKE all things ACCORDING TO THE PATTERN WHICH WAS SHOWN YOU ON THE MOUNTAIN" (Hebrews 8:1-5).

I want you to say three words aloud to yourself: "The true tabernacle." According to the Book of Hebrews, the only true tabernacle is the one set up by the Lord Himself, not by man. Anything else is at best a copy or shadow of the true tabernacle of God.

When Moses was asked to build an earthly copy of the heavenly tabernacle, he found out just how serious God was about His dwelling place and anything built according to its pattern. That is why God warned Moses, "See that you make everything according to the pattern which was shown you on the mountain" (Heb. 8:5). There is a big difference between an exhortation and a warning. Most of us are used to exhortations that basically say, "Try not to mess up." Moses didn't receive an exhortation about the tabernacle. He got an old fashioned warning that said, "*Don't* mess up or else! See that you make everything according to the pattern."

And according to the Law, one may almost say, all things are cleansed with blood, and without shedding of blood there is no forgiveness.

Therefore it was necessary for the copies of the things in the heavens to be cleansed with these, but the heavenly things themselves with better sacrifices than these.

For Christ did not enter a holy place made with hands, a mere copy of the true one, but into heaven itself, now to appear in the presence of God for us;

Nor was it that He should offer Himself often, as the high priest enters the holy place year by year with blood not his own (Hebrews 9:22-25).

If you carefully survey the Old Testament Scriptures, you will see countless copies or types and shadows of true worship appearing from Genesis to Malachi. Even in the New Testament, where we come face to face with the true Messiah foretold and mirrored in the Old Testament, we are dealing with glimpses of heavenly worship that still haven't been manifested or seen on earth. Throughout the Word of God, our heavenly Father is saying something to us about our worship by presenting copy after copy, leading us from type to shadow in our earthly plane to portray in ever-increasing fullness the heavenly pattern, the true worship of the true tabernacle where He resides.

First, let me deal with any doubts you may have about Heaven being a specific place separate from "here." Hebrews 9:24 says, "For Christ did not enter a holy place made with hands, a mere copy of the true one, but *into heaven itself*, now to appear in the presence of God for us." This verse tells us Jesus entered "heaven itself." This verse says the time period that He appears in the presence of God for us is *now*, not "back then" or "someday."

Jesus doesn't have to guess or imagine what Heaven is like because He knows. He dwells there today, right now, at the right hand of the Father. The Holy Spirit knows what real worship is, and He knows what the glory of God is. He knows what's going on in Heaven. But when God talks to us about true worship in Heaven, He must talk to us on our level—which means He must refer us to the taste of earthly praise and worship experiences (like the strawberries in my illustration) to help us somehow grasp the reality of worship on a heavenly plane (the raspberries). He must compare earthly things with heavenly things. That is why we so often hear, "It's something like this. It's like this, but it's not this."

There was a time in Heaven when worship was unflawed throughout the universe. All of the angels—archangels, cherubim, and seraphim—worshiped God together under the leadership of lucifer, the "star of the morning," the covering cherub who was created to be worship leader of the universe. Isaiah the prophet describes lucifer and his fall:

How you have fallen from heaven, O star of the morning, son of the dawn! You have been cut down to the earth, You who have weakened the nations!

*But you said in your heart, "**I will ascend** to heaven; **I will raise** my throne above the stars of God, And **I will sit** on the mount of assembly in the recesses of the north.*

*"**I will** ascend above the heights of the clouds; **I will make** myself like the Most High."*

*Nevertheless **you will be thrust down** to Sheol, to the recesses of the pit* (Isaiah 14:12-15).

I have highlighted the "five wills" that lucifer uttered to himself. He made a crucial mistake along the way by not saying, "I will *if You will*." He didn't involve his Creator because he had ambitions to equal and eclipse his Creator. God answered with a single sentence: "You will not." He said in His Word, "You will be thrust down." I don't know if you realize this, but through the finished work of Jesus Christ, His Son, God has *given* us all five of the things lucifer (now called satan) tried to seize illegally! No wonder he hates us so much!

Another picture of worship in the form of the "chief worshiper" who fell appears in Ezekiel 28. Some misguided artists from past and present have painted pictures of our adversary, satan, depicting him as some kind of grotesque gargoyle. There is no doubt that absolute evil significantly has altered his appearance from what it once was, but even now he has the ability to appear to human eyes as an "angel of light" (2 Cor. 11:14). Consider this picture of what satan once was in the form of lucifer:

> *Son of man, take up a lament concerning the king of Tyre and say to him: "This is what the Sovereign Lord says: 'You were the model of perfection, full of wisdom and perfect in beauty.*
>
> *'You were in Eden, the garden of God; every precious stone adorned you: ruby, topaz and emerald, chrysolite, onyx and jasper, sapphire, turquoise and beryl. Your settings and mountings were made of gold; on the day you were created they were prepared.*
>
> *'You were anointed as a guardian cherub, for so I ordained you. You were on the holy mount of God; you walked among the fiery stones.*
>
> *'You were blameless in your ways from the day you were created till wickedness was found in you.*
>
> *'Through your widespread trade you were filled with violence, and you sinned. So I drove you in disgrace from the*

mount of God, and I expelled you, O guardian cherub, from among the fiery stones.

'Your heart became proud on account of your beauty, and you corrupted your wisdom because of your splendor. So I threw you to the earth; I made a spectacle of you before kings' " (Ezekiel 28:12-17 NIV).

The first thing that comes to your mind after reading this verse might be, "If lucifer was thrown out of Heaven, then how can he have principalities in the "heavenlies"? First of all, there are different "heavens" or levels of the heavens. Solomon declared, "But will God indeed dwell on the earth? *Behold, heaven and the highest heaven* cannot contain Thee, how much less this house which I have built!" (1 Kings 8:27). The apostle Paul wrote, "I know a man in Christ who fourteen years ago—whether in the body I do not know, or out of the body I do not know, God knows—such a man was caught up to the *third heaven*" (2 Cor. 12:2).

Whether you look in the Old Testament or the New, God's Word speaks of heavens in the plural sense. Satan has been removed from the "highest" Heaven where God dwells, but he has not yet been removed from the heavens below the highest realm, the heavenly places.

We read in the Book of Hebrews that "...it was necessary for the copies of the things in the heavens to be cleansed with these, but the heavenly things themselves with *better sacrifices* than these" (Heb. 9:23). Remember that there really is only one Sacrifice—Jesus Christ. We don't need to cleanse the highest Heaven where God dwells because He took care of that a long time ago. We are cleansing the heavens where the warfare is taking place. God wants us to understand that He can accomplish much more through the simplicity of our worship than we realize.

Jesus said, "For where two or three have gathered together in My name, there I am in their midst" (Mt. 18:20).

Let me paraphrase this statement to accurately express the meaning implied in the original Greek manuscript: "If two or three of you *will ever get together*, I will *be so impressed* that *I will come and see it Myself*." Just before Jesus said this, He said something else that is very curious: "Truly I say to you, whatever you shall bind on earth shall be bound in heaven; and whatever you loose on earth shall be loosed in heaven" (Mt. 18:18).

Whenever we try to accomplish earthly things before we have dealt with their counterparts in the heavenlies, we are courting failure. Think of an upside-down tree with its roots in the heavens and its leaves, branches, and fruit on the earth. We're picking the fruit, but we're not dealing with the roots! The issue is this: Can we deal with the roots?

In the Gospel of Luke, Jesus described the way His Father dealt with worthless trees when He said, "And also the axe is already laid at the root of the trees; every tree therefore that does not bear good fruit is cut down and thrown into the fire" (Lk. 3:9). We need to deal with every useless tree in our individual lives in the same way. If we deal with roots of sin, neglect, weakness, bondage, or fear in our lives, we don't have to bother with fruit or outward results of those problems over and over again. If you chop a tree off at its roots, you don't have to ever pick up another seed pod or piece of fruit from that tree.

Many people struggle with recurring problems in their lives because they haven't dealt with the root issues that cause them. As long as you don't deal with root issues, that worthless tree will still bear fruit or spread roots that will affect the good parts of your life.

"You know, I still lose my temper." "I still have these bad thoughts sometimes." "I still get drunk on a number of occasions." "I still hit my wife." Invariably we ask the same question after confessing our recurring problems: "Where is all that coming from?"

The life of every tree is in its roots. If you have a problem or sin that won't go away, then the roots of that "tree" have not been dealt with. As long as the roots of that problem tree are still intact, you will be harvesting more problems from it! Go deal with the root. Strike the root of that tree with the axe of God! You will find the problems that they produced just give way without you ever having to cast out another demon.

Earthly things. Heavenly things. Seen things. Unseen things. Temporal things. Eternal things. Since we tend to look at temporal things all the time, we are too easily disturbed by them. They don't affect God—He affects them! God doesn't manage the world and the universe in nervous fear as He mutters to Himself, "Well, let's see. The communists are in there, so I can only do so much in that place. Oh, the Republicans are in. Let's see, the Democrats are in...." No! God does not manage the universe through the White House, the Kremlin, through Congress or any other parliamentary house of delegates. *He manages it through the Church house* and it's about time the Church realizes it!

"Isn't that a little presumptuous, Pastor?" Absolutely not! According to the Book of Romans:

> *So then it does not depend on the man who wills or the man who runs, but on God who has mercy.*
>
> *For the Scripture says to Pharaoh, "FOR THIS VERY PURPOSE I RAISED YOU UP, TO DEMONSTRATE MY POWER IN YOU, AND THAT MY NAME MIGHT BE PROCLAIMED THROUGHOUT THE WHOLE EARTH."*
>
> *So then He has mercy on whom He desires, and He hardens whom He desires* (Romans 9:16-18).

If you are a blood-washed child of God, you haven't lost your influence in the earth as long as you haven't lost your influence in the heavenlies! Jesus said that whatever we bind in the heavens will be bound on earth. I dearly love the sincere Christian brothers who tell me, "Let's get a conservative Supreme Court in there to get the job done for us. Let's elect so-and-so; he can appoint the right people. That's how we'll get a right decision about abortion."

I just have to tell them: "Forget the Supreme Court! Go where the *real* problem is—declare war in the heavens!" That usually isn't what they want to hear, but I can't get my mind off God's Word in Psalm 149. (Yes, we've read it before, but I'm going to keep taking you to this passage again and again until you're dreaming about it.)

Praise the Lord! Sing to the Lord a new song, and His praise in the congregation of the godly ones.

Let Israel be glad in his Maker; let the sons of Zion rejoice in their King.

Let them praise His name with dancing; let them sing praises to Him with timbrel and lyre.

For the Lord takes pleasure in His people; He will beautify the afflicted ones with salvation.

Let the godly ones exult in glory; let them sing for joy on their beds.

Let the high praises of God be in their mouth, and a two-edged sword in their hand,

To execute vengeance on the nations, and punishment on the peoples;

To bind their kings with chains, and their nobles with fetters of iron;

To execute on them the judgment written; this is an honor for all His godly ones. Praise the Lord! (Psalm 149:1-9)

When the praise of God is in our mouths, what is in our hand? *A two-edged sword.* What is it for? To *inflict vengeance on the nations and punishment on the peoples.* How do we do that? While we praise God with our mouths, we have a two-edged sword in our hands, but meanwhile God gets busy binding their kings with fetters and their nobles with shackles of iron. While we praise God, we are carrying out the sentence of divine judgment written against them. God sums everything up by saying "This is an honor for all His godly ones" (Ps. 149:9).

Let me clarify this because it goes against some of our erroneous presumptions. The glory of the Church is not to be cowering in some corner while we fearfully wait for the rapture to rescue us from the bad old devil. That's not a glory at all, and it is definitely not our glory! Our glory as the Church of the Living God is to be out where the action is. No, I'm not talking about just worshiping God in the cocoon of our four church building walls. I'm talking about a Church that is in the highways and byways, passing out food and giving folks clothing while we tell them with unquenchable joy: "God is not counting your trespasses against you!" That is our glory as saints of the Risen Christ.

Too many Christians have forsaken their God-ordained glory to wring their hands in fear and whine, "The sky is falling!" *Well, it ain't!* (pardon my "Pittsburgh prose"). *The rain is falling!* These are the days of the "latter rain," the prophesied outpouring of the Spirit. God said that in the last days, "I will pour out My Spirit on all mankind" (Joel 2:28). The last time that I checked, the word *all* still meant "all." Don't bother checking the Hebrew—that word still means "all" too![1] If God is pouring out His Spirit on all flesh, can any flesh "duck" it? No. God met them at the womb before they took their first breath and touched their spirits with an inner hunger for His Presence. They have no choice but to accept or reject it.

In a real sense, the nations are controlled by principalities and powers in the heavenly places. It is *our worship* which is the "better sacrifice" that cleanses the heavens! When Jesus appointed 72 people to go into towns and villages ahead of Him, He said, "The harvest is plentiful, but the workers are few" (Mt. 9:37). The Spirit of God has already been poured out on all flesh. That is why the harvest is plenteous. The real battle to bring in the harvest is not with flesh, but with spiritual beings in the heavenlies. That is why the warfare of worship and praise is so important. If you don't have time to preach, if you don't have the opportunity to give your testimony to street people, if you don't have time to receive an offering in a service, then for God's sake, *worship!* Praise God at all costs! More will be accomplished in your praise and worship than could ever happen under the most profound preaching! Your worship and praise releases the unequaled power of God in the heavenlies!

God was looking beyond the copy that Moses was about to build to the real tabernacle of His own choosing when He said: "According to all that I am going to show you, as the pattern of the tabernacle and the pattern of all its furniture, just so you shall construct it" (Ex. 25:9). He was going to invite Moses back up to the mountain so He could show him a pattern of the true sanctuary. What is the point of this sanctuary? He tells Moses in verse 8, "And let them construct a sanctuary for Me, *that I may dwell among them*" (Ex. 25:8).

Jump ahead through the generations to the first chapter of the Gospel of John: "And the Word became flesh, and dwelt among us, and we beheld His glory, glory as of the only begotten from the Father, full of grace and truth" (Jn. 1:14). We called the thing Moses made—the Old Testament copy of a mysterious heavenly original—a "tabernacle" or tent. It was the "tent of His presence" where the Spirit of God Almighty would brood over the ark of the covenant. Do you know what John was saying in the Greek language in

John 1:14? He was saying, "And the Word became flesh and *made His dwelling* [tabernacled!] among us." The King James Version says Jesus "dwelt" among us, and it is the transliteration of the Greek word *skenoo*, a verb form which means "to tent, or encamp, to occupy, to reside or dwell."[2]

This is a more perfect type of the pattern behind the tabernacle Moses made in the Old Testament, but one more step remains before the true pattern is revealed on the earth. It is found in Revelation 21 where John writes:

> *And I saw the holy city, new Jerusalem, coming down out of heaven from God, made ready as a bride adorned for her husband.*
>
> *And I heard a loud voice from the throne, saying, "Behold, the tabernacle of God is among men, and He shall dwell among them, and they shall be His people, and God Himself shall be among them,*
>
> *"And He shall wipe away every tear from their eyes; and there shall no longer be any death; there shall no longer be any mourning, or crying, or pain; the first things have passed away."*
>
> *And He who sits on the throne said, "Behold, I am making all things new"* (Revelation 21:2-5).

Once again, when the writer says that "He shall *dwell* among them," he is using that same tabernacle word, *skenoo*, which refers to pitching a tent or tabernacle in which to dwell. God's aim all along has been to dwell with us in blessed communion.

The old tabernacle of Moses was a man-made tabernacle of skins, but the New Testament tabernacle was in the sinless flesh of the God-man, Jesus Christ (see Jn. 1:14). In the Book of Revelation, it is in us, the people of God, the city of God, the Bride of Christ. God is saying, "I'm going to dwell in you."

And who is this Bride? It's a more complete representation of that which God showed Moses. We are at once earthly, heavenly, temporary, eternal, seen, and unseen. We are the supernatural people of God—redeemed out of the earth from every nation. God wants to cleanse the heavens above the earth with better sacrifices, and we need to bring Him sacrifices that will please Him.

Endnotes

1. *Strong's*, **kol** (H3605), which means "the whole, all, any, or every."

2. *Strong's*, **skenoo** (G4637), "to dwell."

Chapter 9

Worship and the Advance of God's Kingdom

"The best is yet to come."

Three words will mark the imminent doom of any church, any spiritual movement, any denomination, and any spiritual community. Those three fatal words are: "We have arrived."

Our journey from conception to beyond the grave is a journey into an infinite God, so we can never say that we "have arrived" (unless we are admitting that we "have arrived" at the end of ourselves, the end of our strength, and the end of our own abilities). There is just no way a human being can truthfully say, "I know everything there is to know about God." Few of us would say something like this, but many of us *act like it*! There is no way anyone can rightfully say, "I know everything that God is teaching us about some particular thing." The more we know, the more we realize how much we *don't know*. The fact is that we have a perspective of reality that is at best partial.

All of this can be applied to our worship and our praise in one simple phrase: "No matter how good it is, it isn't as good as it can get." By saying "good," I'm not talking about how good it is to or for you. I am talking exclusively about how "good" our worship and praise is to God, who should be the sole object of our worship.

I know we have praise and worship seminars and praise gatherings all around the world. I know they are usually fun to attend and exhilarating to the spirit man. But listen: *It is not for us.* It belongs to God alone, because He alone is worthy to be praised. It is a residual benefit, a "perk," of our family membership as sons and daughters of God through Jesus that we are able to enjoy it, too. Everything we do in our praise and worship should be done for God Almighty. When we lift our hands and voices in praise and worship, it is for God—not just because some man like Joseph L. Garlington said, "Lift your hands." We lift our hands because the Scriptures say, "Lift up your hands to the sanctuary, and bless the Lord" (Ps. 134:2).

I've got some shocking news for you: This "lifting the hands business" isn't a *charismatic* thing—it's a *Bible thing.* Even people who don't want to lift their hands under normal circumstances will do so quickly under certain kinds of pressure. For instance, I may tell everyone, "I will *never* raise my hands at the mere command of man!" But if I walk out the church door and meet a guy with an Uzi (an Israeli submachine gun), I'll pump those hands in the air as fast as I can! The guy probably won't even have to say, "Raise your hands!" Once I see that Uzi, he will have no problems with me. When you raise your hands to God, you are saying, "You will have no problem with me. My life is Yours to command."

What is God leading us to? In a word: *more.* The Book of Proverbs tells us, "The path of the just is as the shining light, that shineth more and more unto the perfect day" (Prov. 4:18 KJV). No matter how much you see, understand, or experience today, God can show you more tomorrow! No matter what you enjoy today, God can give you more to enjoy tomorrow. You may think you have plumbed the depths of your relationship with your spouse, but you haven't. God can show you hidden treasures that you have yet to find in your mate! The same is true of His Word, and of every God-given relationship.

God wants to show us more, give us more, teach us more, build us more, bless us more, challenge us more, and anoint us with more of Himself! There is always *more* in God. Look closely at the way the apostle Paul described the role of the Holy Spirit:

Ye were sealed with that Holy Spirit of promise,

*Which is the **earnest** of our inheritance until the redemption of the purchased possession, unto the praise of His glory* (Ephesians 1:13b-14 KJV).

Even the best things God gives us are precursors of things to come that are even better, richer, fuller, bigger, and deeper than what we have now. Although Jesus Christ won't be "better" than He is now, our understanding of Him, our comprehension of His love and sacrifice, our revelation of Him as God incarnate, and especially *our capacity* to enjoy intimate fellowship with Him will be better, fuller, richer, bigger, and deeper than what we have now.

That is why the apostle Paul called the gift of the indwelling Holy Spirit the "earnest" of our inheritance in Christ. No, he wasn't talking about a down payment. He was talking about "earnest money." If you walk past a used-car lot and linger longer than you intended, a salesperson will ask, "Do you like that car?"

"Yeah, I like that car," you will say.

Then he'll say, "I can hold it for you. Give me some earnest money."

"Would five dollars work?"

"Well, this is a Mercedes," he replies.

"What do you call earnest money?" you ask.

His answer is: "Give me a check for about five hundred bucks—that'll hold it until you come back with the down payment and approved financing." When a salesperson sees a little green, he knows you are really interested.

God gave us the indwelling Holy Spirit as the "earnest" of our eternal inheritance. Now if the Presence of the Holy Spirit in our hearts during our earthly existence isn't even called a "down payment" (which is usually much larger than the amount required for an earnest payment), then what is the magnitude of our inheritance? It is hard to think of the Holy Spirit's indwelling Presence as a gift to kind of tide us over in the earth until we receive "the real thing in its fullness." It makes you wonder what awaits us when we finally get out of these fragile earthly bodies and put on our glorified bodies! Paul wrote in his letter to the Ephesians:

Even when we were dead in our transgressions, [God] made us alive together with Christ (by grace you have been saved),

And raised us up with Him, and seated us with Him in the heavenly places, in Christ Jesus,

*In order that **in the ages to come He might show the surpassing riches of His grace** in kindness toward us in Christ Jesus* (Ephesians 2:5-7).

Do you think you are enjoying the grace of God now? No way. You don't have the facilities to enjoy the immeasurable grace of God. You don't have the "equipment" to enjoy it without measure or limitation. Enjoy what you have received, but always realize that what you have isn't all that He is going to give you! He is telling you through His Word that He is going to give you *more.*

As long as we are earthbound creatures, we are going to be limited in our ability to express everything we feel or perceive in our worship and praise experiences. Right now, as you read these words, if you were trying to express all that you feel, folks around you would probably begin to call you some really strange names. Even the most liberated earthly worshipers are limited in their ability and willingness to offer uninhibited worship to our heavenly Father.

Three structures in the Old Testament deserve our attention because they serve as partial blueprints or rough drawings of the full and rich spiritual worship that we will experience and produce in Heaven. The first structure is called the tabernacle of Moses, because God gave Moses the plans for that tabernacle, or tent of skins, according to the heavenly pattern. The second is called David's tabernacle because it, too, was given to David by God as a copy of the real thing in Heaven. The third is called Solomon's temple. Although it was a fixed structure, the temple was built according to the more complete plans and pattern God gave to Solomon's father, David. There is a fourth structure that may well be included in this list, but we are not going to talk about it in any great length. That is the temple revealed in a vision to the prophet Ezekiel, as recorded in his prophetic book.

The tent or tabernacle of Moses was arranged in the shape of a rectangle with three main sections. The priests entered through one end of the enclosure and passed through the outer court or courtyard past the brazen altar and brazen laver. Within the outer tabernacle stood another enclosure containing the inner court or holy place, and finally the most holy place. Inside the holy place were the table of showbread, the golden altar of incense, and the golden candlestick. Behind these hung a veil or thick tapestry separating the holy of holies from the holy place. It barred physical access and blocked the view of man from the shekinah presence of God under the Old Covenant.

Only the priests (the male descendants of Aaron) and the males of the tribe of Levi were allowed to serve the Lord by offering sacrifices on the brazen altar, or to conduct priestly duties in the vicinity of the holy place. These men began their service at the age of 30 and retired at the age of 50.

The holy of holies was the resting place of the ark of the covenant. The lid of this gold-overlaid ark, featuring two cherubim or covering angels facing each other, overshadowed the mercy seat that hid or covered the law. Placed inside of this ark of the covenant were the Ten Commandments given to Moses, along with Aaron's rod that budded and a pot of manna from the desert wanderings. These three items speak of God's will, authority, and provision, respectively.

Under the law, one person alone was allowed to pass through the veil and see the ark of the covenant once a year. This privilege was reserved for the high priest, and he didn't look or linger very long. This priest would fearfully pass through the veil once a year on the day of atonement to sprinkle blood on the mercy seat seven times and purge, or atone for, the sins of the nation for one more year.

Let me skip past David's tabernacle for a moment to look at Solomon's temple. If the tabernacle built by Moses cost the Israelites a couple million dollars, then Solomon's temple cost about four billion, one-hundred million dollars! That temple would make the Rev. Schuller's Crystal Cathedral look like Swiss cheese in terms of the investment that was made. I believe Rev. Schuller's congregation invested between 14 and 17 million dollars in that facility in Anaheim, California.

Amos the prophet said, "Surely the Lord God does nothing unless He reveals His secret counsel to His servants the prophets" (Amos 3:7). God is constantly forecasting His plan, our destiny, and future events throughout the Scriptures. Yes, even the Old Testament gives prophecies about what is going to take place in our day. From time to time, I like to share a little poem about the Old and New Testaments or

Covenants of the Bible: "The Old is in the New explained. The New is in the Old contained. The Old is in the New revealed. The New is in the Old concealed."

Unfortunately, much confusion has been created by the decision by some church leaders to lump together many of the prophecies in the Old and New Testaments and stick them into a theological "never-never land" called the Millennium, where we are forbidden to enjoy those things right now.

Sandwiched between the badger-skin tabernacle of Moses and the ornate masterpiece of Solomon's temple is David's tabernacle. Each of these structures was a copy of something that is true; they were not phony. Their only problem was they were deficient in their ability to reflect the real. The tabernacle, the ark of the covenant, and all of the other elements of these structures are types and shadows of the Lord Jesus Christ in one way or another. I most want to talk about David's tabernacle. The reason is found, oddly enough, in a New Testament passage reporting statements by James the apostle in the Book of Acts citing an older prophecy from the Book of Amos!

> *Simeon has related how God first concerned Himself about taking from among the Gentiles a people for His name.*
>
> *And with this the words of the Prophets agree, just as it is written,*
>
> *"AFTER THESE THINGS I will return, AND I WILL REBUILD THE TABERNACLE OF DAVID WHICH HAS FALLEN, AND I WILL REBUILD ITS RUINS, AND I WILL RESTORE IT,*
>
> *"IN ORDER THAT THE REST OF MANKIND MAY SEEK THE LORD, AND ALL THE GENTILES WHO ARE CALLED BY MY NAME,"*

SAYS THE LORD, WHO MAKES THESE THINGS KNOWN FROM OF OLD (Acts 15:14-18).

The Church in the Book of Acts encountered some basic problems early in its existence because its leaders viewed the church as an offshoot of the Jewish faith—at best, a Jewish church. They didn't really embrace Jesus' command to, "go into all the world, beginning at Jerusalem and Judea and Samaria, into the uttermost parts." They figured (and the Book of Acts demonstrates this) that Jesus' words were a command to seek out Jews in these places. They enjoyed the Holy Spirit and began to "camp" where they were. And, they liked it there. In the end, God had to motivate them by persecution to go on, to scatter the gospel message outside of the holy city of Jerusalem. Eventually, the First Century believers did venture out or were driven out of Jerusalem and into the byways of international society.

The problem was that the Jewish disciples really weren't convinced that the gospel message was for Gentiles as well as Jews—even though Jesus and the prophets of old specifically said this on many occasions. They preferred, instead, to stay among their own people. That's when God spoke to Peter in a vision and sent him to the house of an Italian Gentile named Cornelius. Peter and his seven companions were shocked when the Holy Ghost fell on Cornelius' household right in the middle of Peter's message. I can almost see Peter look at his Jewish friends for a reaction when the Gentiles started speaking in other tongues: "Look, guys, I didn't have anything to do with that. I was just talking...You guys saw me—I didn't put my hands on anybody, right? Right?"

Even after Peter and his seven witnesses returned to Jerusalem to say, "Look, it was a sovereign move of the Holy Spirit. Gentiles are now coming into the Kingdom," the Jewish church leaders still said, "Well, we're not sure that this is God." It was God, and it still is God!

When Paul and Barnabas began to aggressively share the good news with the Gentiles, they responded to Christ by the thousands, and the Holy Spirit moved among them. That left the Jews wondering, "Well, what should we do with them? Should we circumcise them and make them Jewish believers like us? Should we bring them into the law?" Acts 15 is the record of the first church council called in Jerusalem to decide this issue. It was at the conclusion of this council when James said that God took "from among the Gentiles a people for His name" and that He was determined to rebuild David's fallen tabernacle (Acts 15:14).

Why is God going to restore David's ancient tabernacle? Isn't it just an Old Covenant type and shadow of a New Testament reality? God Himself answers this question in Acts 15:

"AFTER THESE THINGS I will return, AND I WILL REBUILD THE TABERNACLE OF DAVID WHICH HAS FALLEN, AND I WILL REBUILD ITS RUINS, AND I WILL RESTORE IT,

"IN ORDER THAT THE REST OF MANKIND MAY SEEK THE LORD, AND ALL THE GENTILES WHO ARE CALLED BY MY NAME,"

SAYS THE LORD, WHO MAKES THESE THINGS KNOWN FROM OF OLD (Acts 15:16-18).

God has known what He was going to do from the beginning of time. There isn't a thing going on right now that has taken God by surprise. He knows who will be President of the United States in the next five elections, He knows where every nuclear warhead is stored, and He knows the name and address of every criminal on this planet. God's chief concern is extending His Kingdom. The future is not a problem to God, and it shouldn't be a problem to you.

I'm interested in the tabernacle of David because James the apostle, speaking under the inspiration of the Holy

Spirit, quoted Amos the prophet and said, "*In that day* I will restore David's fallen tent." James was publicly announcing "that day" had come, and the baptism of the Holy Spirit among the Gentiles marked the beginning of the fulfillment of the prophesy of Amos. The last days began with the outpouring of the Holy Spirit on the day of Pentecost as Joel prophesied centuries before, a fact Peter mentioned in his address to the large crowd of Jews after the upper room experience (see Acts 2:16).

I think we need to find out everything we can about what the tabernacle of David is and what it is to be in our day! We need to start with the prophecy of Amos:

> "*In that day I will raise up the fallen booth of David, and wall up its breaches; I will also raise up its ruins, and rebuild it as in the days of old;*
>
> "*That they may possess the remnant of Edom and all the nations who are called by My name," declares the Lord who does this.*
>
> "*Behold, days are coming," declares the Lord, "when the plowman will overtake the reaper and the treader of grapes him who sows seed; when the mountains will drip sweet wine, and all the hills will be dissolved*" (Amos 9:11-13).

The "last days" began at Pentecost nearly two millenniums ago. In our day, "the plowman will overtake the reaper and the treader of grapes him who sows seed; when the mountains will drip sweet wine..." (Amos 9:13). God is talking about *unprecedented fruitfulness* here. He is saying that there will be so much to reap for the Kingdom that the plowman will be right behind the reaper to urge him, as he says, "Come on, man. You're holding us up!"

If you look closely at a map comparing the size of Judah and Israel when David first ascended their thrones to the size of the reunited Israel at the height of his reign, you will see that those borders were extended in an unprecedented expansion on every side. Ironically, although David's son, Solomon, stepped onto the throne equipped with incredible wisdom, almost unlimited wealth, and the most powerful standing army in Asia Minor (thanks to the success of his warrior father and the grace of God), Solomon did nothing to expand his borders further. In fact, his sin led to the division of the throne again and the downfall of Israel in the end. After David died, Israel lost ground and never regained it.

The reason for David's success was the unprecedented worship and praise going on during his life and reign! (And Solomon's failure stems from its replacement with rote ritual in the temple made of stone.)

When you read David's account in Psalm 149 of using praise to bind the nobles and their princes with fetters and chains, you can almost hear David saying: "Guys, there's some more land right over there, and it is part of our inheritance. Let's worship and praise the Lord, and then go claim our land." David and his followers used praise to God to "push out" or expand their borders.

Yet, even David experienced serious ups and downs in his zeal to perfect praise and dwell in God's Presence. Like many worshipers and worship leaders today, David made the fatal mistake of trying to do the work of God outside of God's guidelines or blessing in Second Samuel.

Now David again gathered all the chosen men of Israel, thirty thousand.

And David arose and went with all the people who were with him to Baale-judah, to bring up from there the ark of God which is called by the Name, the very name of the Lord of hosts who is enthroned above the cherubim.

And they placed the ark of God on a new cart that they might bring it from the house of Abinadab which was on the

*hill; and Uzzah and Ahio, the sons of Abinadab, were lead-
ing the new cart.*

*So they brought it with the ark of God from the house of Abi-
nadab, which was on the hill; and Ahio was walking ahead
of the ark.*

*Meanwhile, David and all the house of Israel were celebrat-
ing before the Lord with all kinds of instruments made of fir
wood, and with lyres, harps, tambourines, castanets and
cymbals.*

*But when they came to the threshing floor of Nacon, Uzzah
reached out toward the ark of God and took hold of it, for
the oxen nearly upset it.*

*And the anger of the Lord burned against Uzzah, and God
struck him down there for his irreverence; and he died there
by the ark of God.*

*And David became angry because of the Lord's outburst
against Uzzah, and that place is called Perez-uzzah to this
day.*

*So David was afraid of the Lord that day; and he said,
"How can the ark of the Lord come to me?"* (2 Samuel
6:1-9).

When David's men set the ark of God on a "new cart," it's
too bad they didn't hear someone say, "Uh-oh." It would
have saved them a lot of grief. David seemed to be doing a
good thing with a good motive—the problem was that his
method wasn't so good. He was operating in ignorance because he hadn't consulted God's Word. Yes, David and all of
Israel were worshiping God with all their might with songs,
harps, lyres, tambourines, and cymbals. That was good.

The problem was the new cart. When the procession
came to the threshing floor of Nacon, a priest named Uzzah
reached out to steady the rocking ark of God, and God
struck him down for his presumption. Right there, in the

midst of exuberant worship and praise, a man died literally in the shadow of the ark of God. David became angry at God for killing Uzzah, but the real culprit was a little closer to home. David's presumption had caused Uzzah's death. Suddenly, we find that David was *afraid* of the Lord. We need to understand that the "fear of the Lord" is one of the missing elements that God will restore to His Church in our day.

David basically dropped the ark of the Lord like a hot potato and left it standing on the threshing floor of Obed-edom the Gittite. Yet God wanted to teach David something about His Presence, and the proper way to approach and reverence Him—even in his methodology of worship! David needed to learn to honor God in *God's way* to receive the approval of God. When God showered Obed-edom with blessings, David knew he had to swallow his pride and once again try to bring the ark into Jerusalem. Notice how he did it:

*And David went and brought up the ark of God from the house of Obed-edom into the city of David **with gladness**.*

And so it was, that when the bearers of the ark of the Lord had gone six paces, he sacrificed an ox and a fatling.

And David was dancing before the Lord with all his might, and David was wearing a linen ephod (2 Samuel 6:12b-14).

It was at this point that David's wife (Saul's daughter) Michal peered out of her window and despised David because he was leaping and dancing in public celebration over the blessings of God without inhibition or any thought about the approval of other people. Michal should have been rejoicing over the glory of the Lord returning to Israel, but, instead, she was groveling in the dust of her own jealousy and petty bitterness over her husband's devotion to God. Her anointed husband literally was walking toward the door of their home to pronounce a *blessing* on his household when Michal stepped out to meet him and spew her bitter ridicule over him. I believe she was caught off guard by his response.

Michal probably believed her ridicule would reduce David and pull him down to her level, but he fired back with authoritative affirmations of God's blessings and decrees over his life. Then he defiantly declared his intention to be a fool for God's sake, no matter what the cost. Michal's curse over David was turned aside by the greater truth of God's pleasure in David as a worshiper and obedient servant. David's blessing never came to Michal, and neither did God's. She died childless and bitter, while her husband died in God's favor, surrounded by his children (by other wives) and the fruits of a lifetime of worship before God. It is just the same today when critics focus their energies on criticizing the things of God and the people who yield themselves to the Lord. The critics' negative rejection of the holy things of God will cost them in the end, but the true worshipers and obedient servants will enjoy the bountiful fruit of their labor.

The second time around, David discarded the new cart and called for the Levites—the tribe chosen by God to bear the ark of His Presence. They carried the ark of the Lord to the hill in Jerusalem called "the city of David" (which was called Mount Zion until David's men captured it by defeating the Jebusites) and placed it inside a tent that King David had pitched for it. Inside what? The tent (tabernacle) that David had pitched for it.

David broke precedent again when he personally offered burnt offerings and peace offerings to the Lord. Then he blessed the people in the name of the Lord Almighty and gave everyone a loaf of bread, a cake of dates, and a cake of raisins before they returned to their homes.

Whatever you do, you need to understand you cannot be a worshiper and a man-pleaser at the same time. If you're going to please God, then be prepared to be humiliated before your peers at some point. Why? Because the word *worship* doesn't just mean "to sing." It also means "to prostrate yourself" and "to bow down." That's worship, and that can be embarrassing when you are surrounded by critics who don't want anybody to be more "spiritual" than they are. One of the most common (and accurate) statements that we hear these days is: "It seems as though every previous move of the Holy Spirit, no matter what kind of move it is, persecutes the next move." If you examine church history, you will see just how true this is.

The Anabaptists, who believed baptism was only for those old enough to knowingly confess their sin and allegiance to Christ, were persecuted by the Calvinists, who were offended by this practice. The Calvinists practiced infant baptism. They told the Anabaptists, "Do you want to be baptized? We'll baptize you!" Then, they would take their victims out to a lake or river, wrap heavy weights around them, and drop them in the water to drown.

The current renewal movement was persecuted in a number of ways by other groups who are now saying, "I'm hungry for something." What they are hungry for is the very thing that they have persecuted in recent years. I've learned that when people get real hungry, they will say, "I don't care. I am hungry. Whatever it is that God wants, that's what I want." Spiritual hunger will motivate us to reach out to God in ways that move us beyond our limited perception of ourselves.

Worship is designed to move you out of self-consciousness into God-consciousness (and this can be an interesting journey). Yet true worship always demands a price of us.

Part IV

The Tabernacle of David

Chapter 10

David's Tabernacle of Praise and Worship

King David, the prophet, priest, and king of Israel is God's preeminent model for worship in Scripture. If you want to know how to worship, look at David. If you want to know how to praise God, you can learn from David.

In the previous chapter, we learned that God wants to put *something* back in the Church. He intends to do it by rebuilding David's tabernacle of praise and worship. This reminds me of the stacks of "enriched bread" found in grocery stores across America. Years ago, we didn't need "enriched" bread because we made it fresh each day at home by using whole grain flour that was freshly milled down the road.

Nowadays, we "process" our wheat before we use it because we are modern people. That means we use machines to knock off the good stuff like bran. We grind and bleach what's left until no vitamins or nutrients remain in the flour to mess up the bland taste that we've come to crave. Finally, we add liberal amounts of "dough softeners and conditioners," and just before we bake the stuff, we use machines to squirt a vitamin mixture back into the gooey paste. That allows us to proudly slap an "enriched bread" label on the package so people can spread peanut butter, honey, and jelly on the bland stuff and say, "Yum, yum. Enriched bread." But it's not.

That's exactly what happened to our worship. The ex-worship leader of the universe slipped into the Church and said: "I'll take those raucous horns. (They can't be holy. They're the traditional instruments of warfare. Nope, you don't need those disturbing your services.) I'll definitely take those noisy drums off your hands, and give me those cymbals—you don't need them. Oh, I've got to have the guitars—they sound so good, they've got to be sinful, right? Okay, now. What are we left with? Oh yeah, this is what I want you to sing. Mmmmmm. It sounds nice and religious and b-o-r-...oops. Yes, monotone is good. Ahh, nice and lethargic, uh, I mean worshipful. Now whatever you do, don't put any passion or emotion in your worship and praise music, because you know those are bad. Mmm, mmm." (A snore is heard in the background).

Then, the church people asked, *"What's that?"*

"Oh, well," the helpful ex-worship leader said, *"That's true worship—the kind I find well-pleasing to my soul."*

For centuries, God's people have been passing by the devil's bistros, pubs, bars, and taverns that are just jamming with the most powerful sounds imaginable. You feel attracted to the music, but guilt strikes and the devil strikes home with the comment, "That's the devil's music." In each generation, our kids have passed the same sounds coming out of those joints, only to plop down in dull church services where they hear sleepy people intone monotonous hymns to the joyless sounds of "mmmm, mmmmm, mmmm." When our kids meet their friends, it is a relief to finally be around some music that speaks to the hormones, energy, and optimism boiling up in their blood. But when we say, "Let's go to church," they can't help but say, "Oh, Dad, it's dull over there. Nobody's happy at church. Why is that?"

God wants to give us something that we processed out in our modern sophistication and wisdom. The devil understands the power of music, but the Church has been so ignorant over the centuries that it has freely given away what God intended to be its exclusive domain. We're just now beginning to understand the power God invested in music. God is saying to us, "Get with it!"

David was ahead of his time. He delved so deeply into the depths of worship that he crossed the barrier of time into New Covenant intimacy with God—intimacy that transcended the law! We need today what David had back then, but our problem is we are afraid of "new" things. We like the old, even if God isn't "speaking that language" anymore. When someone dares to introduce something fresh that the Holy Spirit is doing, strong opposition will present itself—especially from those who experienced a move of the Holy Spirit just before this one.

How do I stay flexible, in terms of being a wineskin? How can I remain flexible and turn my old wineskin into a new wineskin? I need to soak the old wineskin in water and beat it with rocks. I want to stay flexible, I want to be new, but it will cost me to stay flexible.

David introduced something that was born of the Spirit and moved simultaneously with another wineskin! David's tabernacle was patterned after the tabernacle of Moses and enriched with David's rich intimate relationship with God, a relationship nurtured through decades of praise on the hillsides with the sheep and in the cave of Adullam in desperate times. David freely borrowed from Moses and established something new that God is using to enrich His Church today! And he did it without despising the tabernacle of Moses. In other words, "You need to keep a good attitude about where you came from."

Remember the concluding words of James the apostle in Acts 15 when he quoted Amos the prophet:

"AFTER THESE THINGS I will return, AND I WILL REBUILD THE TABERNACLE OF DAVID WHICH HAS FALLEN, AND I WILL REBUILD ITS RUINS, AND I WILL RESTORE IT,

"IN ORDER THAT THE REST OF MANKIND MAY SEEK THE LORD, AND ALL THE GENTILES WHO ARE CALLED BY MY NAME,"

SAYS THE LORD, WHO MAKES THESE THINGS KNOWN FROM OF OLD (Acts 15:16-18).

God wants us to understand that just because something is new to us does not mean it is new to Him. He gives us things in relationship to His time and season for introducing it back to the Church. He is giving us back something that we had lost. When we see something in the Scriptures that we never saw before, the truth is that it was there all the time!

The Old Testament prophets, Amos and Joel, spoke of God's mighty works "in that day," but it is abundantly clear that "that day" is now! We live in "that day." Some of the prophecies were fulfilled in the thirtieth year of Jesus' earthly ministry when He read from Isaiah's scroll the ancient prophecy that says, "THE SPIRIT OF THE LORD IS UPON ME, BECAUSE HE ANOINTED ME TO PREACH THE GOSPEL…" and then declared, "Today this Scripture has been fulfilled in your hearing" (Lk. 4:18,21).

Some of the ancient prophecies came to pass on the cross when Jesus declared, "It is finished" (Jn. 19:30), and others came to pass on the day of Pentecost when the Holy Spirit descended like fire on the 120 in the upper room (see Acts 2:1-4). Jesus told the disciples, "I have many more things to say to you, but you cannot bear them now" (Jn. 16:12).

But Jesus knows our frame and our limitations. There is a whole lot of truth that the Church wasn't able to embrace historically. But now He is restoring many things to us because more and more believers are praying, "God, I'm hungry for something more than what I've had! I want more of You!" God's answer to our prayer is the restoration of David's fallen tabernacle or tent of praise and true worship.

One of the things undergirding the expansion of the Kingdom of God is a new concept of praise. Something mighty is taking place in the earth. Praise and worship are at the center of what is happening. I can stand in our worship facility in Pittsburgh, Pennsylvania, and join with other believers with uplifted hands and affect nations! The shock wave of our praise is unaffected by distance, different time zones, or different languages, cultures, and political systems. It is a spiritual force to be reckoned with, and the Church is just now catching on to this truth.

David's earthly kingdom expanded phenomenally, and it cannot be attributed to anything other than his commitment to worship and praise. David was a "praise animal." He knew how to do it right. What do you think Jesus, the prophetic "son of David" was? He was a worshiper; He understood the power and importance of praise to His Father. That is why He told the Samaritan woman at the well, "May I tell you that the Father is not looking for apostles? He is not looking for prophets and evangelists either. God is a spirit, and He is looking for real worshipers who will worship Him in spirit and in truth" (my paraphrase of John 4:23).

The central focal point in Old Testament worship was the ark of the covenant, on which the cherubim overshadowed the mercy seat. It was universally considered to be the most significant piece of furniture in the tabernacle because it was the ark of the covenant of the Lord. David not only erected a tent and recruited the Levites to transport the ark to the tabernacle, but he also prepared an atmosphere and offering of praise and worship to welcome and bless the Lord of the ark. "Then David spoke to the chiefs of the Levites to appoint their relatives the singers, with instruments of music, harps, lyres, loud-sounding cymbals, to raise sounds of joy" (1 Chron. 15:16). The Bible record also tells us David had high standards for leadership in service to the Lord: "And Chenaniah, chief of the Levites, was in charge of the singing; he gave instruction in singing *because he was skillful*" (1 Chron. 15:22).

David organized the Levites to minister regularly before the ark of the covenant according to each day's requirements, but things seemed odd about the whole arrangement—this was radically different from the worship offered at the tabernacle of Moses. Where was the ark of the covenant during this time? It rested in the place David had prepared for it, on the little hill formerly called Mount Zion, now called "the city of David." The holy ark of the covenant was simply covered with a tent—it was not blocked out or concealed from view. The tent was only extensive enough to protect the ark from natural elements like rain, heavy dew, and the sun's rays. If you remember, the tabernacle of Moses had three layers of shielding separating the shekinah presence of God from the common people.

When the ark of the covenant was in Moses' tabernacle, it was completely concealed in the holy of holies. Only one person was permitted to enter that room once a year. David's tabernacle also had an area called the holy of holies, and in every other respect, besides the mostly open tent design, the patterns established in the tabernacle of Moses were followed (see 1 Chron. 16:39-40)—with *one incredible difference*.

The Book of Second Samuel also describes the return of the ark to Jerusalem, while adding another bit of information that marks the most significant change in worship since the day God spoke to Moses about the ark of the covenant. David told Nathan about his desire to build God "a house," and Nathan at first told him to do it. When God reprimanded the prophet, he returned to tell David that God would not allow him to build a house for Him, but He would build David's house. At that point, the Scriptures say, "Then David the king *went in and sat* before the Lord, and he said, 'Who am I, O Lord God, and what is my house, that Thou hast brought me this far?' " (2 Sam. 7:18).

Now what did David do? He *sat before the Lord*! Where did he do that? He did it *in front of the ark of the covenant, in the holy of holies.*

David was not a priest in the line of Aaron, nor was he a Levite. Yet, here he was sitting in the presence of God. Keep in mind that under the law, only the Levites were allowed to serve in the holy place. Only the high priest was allowed to enter the most holy place with the ark of the covenant to offer sacrifice once a year. What we see here is that David represents a *greater priesthood*, a type and shadow of the coming Messiah which is confirmed in the Book of Hebrews:

> *For when the priesthood is changed, of necessity there takes place a change of law also.*
>
> *For the one concerning whom these things are spoken belongs to another tribe, from which no one has officiated at the altar.*
>
> *For it is evident that our Lord was descended from Judah, a tribe with reference to which Moses spoke nothing concerning priests.*
>
> *And this is clearer still, if another priest arises according to the likeness of Melchizedek,*
>
> *Who has become such not on the basis of a law of physical requirement, but according to the power of an indestructible life* (Hebrews 7:12-16).

David was unknowingly demonstrating that a greater priesthood was coming, a priesthood rooted in relationship, not mere ritual or ancestral lineage. We have become a kingdom of priests and kings in Christ before God. David was a type and shadow of the better priesthood to come. God was building a house—the house of David—whose Seed, Jesus Christ, would tear down the dividing walls so every man and woman could sit and gaze at the beauty of the Lord's Presence.

The psalms of David reveal a totally new concept of abiding in God's Presence, of dwelling in His tabernacle and temple in complete peace and safety. This man *knew* and *loved* God with all of his heart; he didn't simply fear Him from a distance. God didn't want to insulate Himself from David, because He had found a man after His own heart. Law isn't needed where there is love and devotion. In Psalm 27, David described some of the enemies and dangers he faced, when he said:

> *One thing have I asked from the Lord, that I shall seek: that I may dwell in the house of the Lord all the days of my life, to behold the beauty of the Lord, and to meditate in His temple.*

> *For in the day of trouble He will conceal me in His tabernacle; in the secret place of His tent He will hide me; He will lift me up on a rock.*

> *And now my head will be lifted up above my enemies around me; and I will offer in His tent sacrifices with shouts of joy; I will sing, yes, I will sing praises unto the Lord (Psalm 27:4-6).*

Have you noticed that in this tabernacle, you don't need to bring a burnt offering. You give the Lord shouts of joy as a sacrifice. You sacrifice shouts of joy to Him. David is describing an intimate, loving, and confident relationship with the living God—a relationship never seen in the earth up to that point in human history. Some leaders were allowed to commune with God, but never on such an intimate and loving level. David's precedent-setting relationship with God would be unequaled and unparalleled until the arrival of Jesus Christ. The power of his praise and worship is still being restored to the Church today!

The circumstances surrounding David's life when he wrote this psalm should encourage anyone who feels surrounded and alone! An evil man was advancing to devour David's flesh; David was facing antagonistic armies with war breaking out against him. In the middle of all this, David said, "I'm looking in the tabernacle, I'm inquiring in the beauty of the Lord, and I'm saying, God, 'Isn't this wonderful?' " David is saying, "When the enemy comes to eat up my flesh, I go to the table and look at God" (see Psalm 23).

Something is special about the sanctuary or dwelling place of God. According to Psalm 73, when the writer got fed up with evil people prospering while holy people suffered, he headed for the sanctuary of God. He admits, "When I pondered to understand this, it was troublesome in my sight until I came into the sanctuary of God..." (Ps. 73:16-17a).

Why did David go to the tabernacle, the sanctuary of God after his disappointing meeting with Nathan? He did it to get God's perspective on things. *Worship helps you get your perspective right!* It is easy to get down when you look at drug pushers making fortunes overnight by selling men's souls and when you look at all of the corruption in politics. You have a choice at that point: You can either get down, or you can get to the tabernacle and sanctuary of God. Something happens when you behold God's shekinah glory and the beauty of His Presence. Like Asaph, the author of Psalm 73, we can say, "[When] I came into the sanctuary of God; then I perceived their end" (Ps. 73:17).

God is looking for a resting place. He will take pleasure in your house if He finds you praising and worshiping Him in your home. What do you think He does when He hears you worshiping in the morning: "I love you, Lord. I worship and bless You. Lord, I love You and I want to sit at Your feet and tell You how good You are and how much You mean to me"?

I can almost *hear* God say, "You know, I'll just rest here for awhile. I've been looking for a house like this all morning!"

We need to do what David did so well in Psalm 132:8 when he said, "Arise, O Lord, to Thy resting place; Thou and the ark of Thy strength." Then he said, "Let Thy priests be clothed with righteousness; and let Thy godly ones sing for joy" (Ps. 132:9). Now look closely at some of the verses that follow this in Psalm 132:

For the Lord has chosen Zion; He has desired it for His habitation.

"This is My resting place forever; here I will dwell, for I have desired it.

"I will abundantly bless her provision; I will satisfy her needy with bread.

"Her priests also I will clothe with salvation; and her godly ones will sing aloud for joy.

"There I will cause the horn of David to spring forth; I have prepared a lamp for Mine anointed" (Psalm 132:13-17).

Don't miss out on what I'm going to say to you: Many of us begin to panic when we start to run out of the necessities of life or the things we need to minister or reach out to others. But, if we ever get our act together and *prepare a place for God's presence* in Zion, then God will provide all of our needs! Jesus echoed this even more powerfully in Matthew 6:33 when He said, "But seek first His kingdom and His righteousness; and all these things shall be added to you." Get to

Zion. Get to the tabernacle and sit in the place where God finds rest.

I believe this Scripture is saying, "Worship and prosperity are not divorced from one another." God has promised that He will abundantly bless your provision! If you've been complaining, try praise. If you've been murmuring, try worship. If God hasn't shown up because you've been bellyaching, then see if He'll show up when you get to the tabernacle of David and begin to offer sacrifices of joy. Once you've learned to sit in the tabernacle of God and create an atmosphere of praise, it is time to move on, move up to new levels of divinely creative praise and worship.

Chapter 11

A New Song

We have an altar, from which those who serve the tabernacle have no right to eat...For here we do not have a lasting city, but we are seeking the city which is to come. Through [Jesus] then, let us continually offer up a sacrifice of praise to God... *(Hebrews 13:10,14,15a).*

While our Savior is the same yesterday, today, and forever (according to Hebrews 13:8), our understanding of God and the worship we offer to Him *is changing*! We still are learning about worship. Though it won't be perfected in our time (as we discussed briefly in an earlier chapter), we are sure to express it with greater depth and maturity the more we walk in obedience to the Holy Spirit.

Perfect worship will only take place when we are in a perfect atmosphere and environment, worshiping with perfect bodies and sensibilities. Right now, in our day, God is equipping and preparing us for all that He will do in the ages to come. That is why He is rebuilding the fallen tabernacle of David. King David possessed *something* in his praise and worship life that God is determined to see restored to His Church (because He likes it).

You can't talk about David's tabernacle without talking about a new sound, a new sacrifice, and a new song. These things are like the precious treasures Jesus described to the disciples in the Gospel of Matthew after sharing several parables on the Kingdom of Heaven:

> *"Have you understood all these things?" They said to Him, "Yes."*
>
> *And He said to them, "Therefore every scribe who has become a disciple of the kingdom of heaven is like a head of a household, who brings forth out of his treasure things new and old" (Matthew 13:51-52).*

Is the old always bad because it's old? Absolutely not! I can remember singing, "Oh magnify the Lord with me, ye people of His choice; let all to whom He lendeth breath now in His Name rejoice. For love's blessed revelation, for rest from condemnation, for uttermost salvation to Him give thanks. Let all the people praise Thee, let all the people praise Thee, let all the people praise Thy Name forever and forever more, forever more dear Lord." That is a wonderful song. I can remember singing that song at our former pastorate, Rehobeth Church in Washington, D.C., at 8th and L Streets—singing until there was no more juice in it!

When I first came into the Charismatic Renewal in the early 1970s, no good songs were out there by today's standards. A lot of the early Charismatic praise songs were little more than rhymed formula tunes: "He died for me, upon the tree, and by His grace He set me free." They weren't musical—at least to me. They just weren't my "genre," if you know what I mean. However, we were trying to do a new thing and enter new levels in our spiritual walk with God. It takes time, effort, and experience to develop new music to express our new experiences in God.

When things are evolving or changing, we are often tempted to look back on our beginnings and despise the days of our changing process. "Oh man, I can't believe we used to sing that song." I can honestly tell you that in the early days of the Renewal, we took great delight in singing songs with lyrics like, "Peter walked on the water; Moses walked on dry land; Jonah sank to the bottom, and landed on the sand. I'm walking on the water, holding Jesus' hand, and I know that someday He's going to walk me to the promised, walk me to the promised, walk me to the promised land." It doesn't do anything for me now, but it meant a lot back then.

Jesus said that any Bible student who studied the Kingdom of Heaven would be like a householder who "brings forth out of his treasure things new and old" (Mt. 13:52). Now, why do we combine old things with new things? Because people are also uncomfortable with new things. Jesus said:

> *But new wine must be put into fresh wineskins. And no one, after drinking old wine wishes for new; for he says, "The old is good enough"* (Luke 5:38-39).

Most of us don't say, "This is great!" when something new is introduced. We usually sit there in disapproving shock. I heard a Christian leader named John Pool quote a passage from Luke's Gospel and say, "The children of this world are in their generation wiser than the children of light" (see Lk. 16:8) to illustrate our blindness to the need for adaptation, change, and creativity.

Martin Luther said of his generation, "I need a way to capture the minds of people." That determination, mixed with prayer, led Luther—who had not always been a saved, sanctified, filled-with-the-Holy Ghost monk—to "borrow" a popular bar song of the day and fit it with a new set of lyrics based on some powerful passages of Scripture. Today we recognize this "revered classic of the Church," sung to the tune of a "Top-40" beer-guzzling song, as "A Mighty Fortress is Our God"!

Now that is a great song, but many people don't know that this song—universally reverenced as a bastion of conservative sacred musicology—is a reworked common tavern song. Martin Luther dared to make the leap from the Gregorian chants that had dominated Church music for centuries. Martin Luther piggybacked substantive, theologically sound words with the popular musical melodies of the common man in his generation. It worked. People around the world began to sing the Word of God, and Martin Luther was able to grab the hearts and minds of his generation with a revolutionary product of the age. The same thing happened in the ministry of the Wesley brothers during the Great Awakening, when many of our popular hymns of the church were created by using popular melodies common in pubs and taverns across England and the United States.

In our day, stuffy folks in churches from coast to coast are saying, "Well, they need to keep that rap and hip-hop music out of here. And, the alternative stuff is too alternative for me. We'll do just fine with the sacred classics my grandfather loved to sing, like 'A Mighty Fortress Is Our God.'"

Now, rap music and hip-hop isn't my thing, but it is (or was) the music of this generation. This music moves so fast that it's hard to keep track of trends these days. This fact is absolutely true: *If the Church doesn't learn how to be wise in its generation, it will lose its generation.*

If it was possible for a new sound to emerge in God's Kingdom in David's day, in the days of Martin Luther, and the Wesley's day, is God doing something new now? As always, I can guarantee you there are people who would shake their heads "no" before I even finish this sentence. In the 1800s, a prominent church leader publicly expressed the fear that all of the music "would be used up" because there were only a "finite number of notes." This leader confidently warned his listeners that if they weren't careful, all of the music would be gone! Of course, that was before the arrival of Ralph Carmichael, Andréa Crouch, Sandi Patty, Gene Ghets, Stan Kenton, Count Basie, and Duke Ellington. The worst thing we can do is to sit back in our isolated perspective and say, "This is it. We've arrived." We've barely started!

"Meanwhile, David and all the house of Israel were celebrating before the Lord with all kinds of instruments made of fir wood, and with lyres, harps, tambourines, castanets and cymbals" (2 Sam. 6:5). How were they celebrating? "With all their might." Where? "Before the Lord." With what? "With songs, with harps, with lyres, tambourines, with castanets and cymbals." How many? "David and all the house of Israel." That's a lot of people, isn't it?

What do you do "before the Lord" with your family and local church body? Do you sit and endure with a minimum investment of energy and a low tolerance for anything different that involves change? Or, would I see you worship God with all your might with a bead of sweat rising across your forehead? I have to warn you that your answer may be self-incriminating....

God's Word declares in both the New and Old Testaments, "And you shall love the Lord your God with all your heart, and with all your soul, and with all your mind, and with all your strength" (Mk. 12:30; Mt. 22:37; Lk. 10:27; Deut. 6:5). This verse defines beyond any argument the *intensity levels* of true, biblical worship and devotion to God.

The Book of First Chronicles says something unusual about the *content, scale, and format* of worship in David's day. Is God about to restore these to the Church in our day?

Now when David reached old age, he made his son Solomon king over Israel.

And he gathered together all the leaders of Israel with the priests and the Levites.

And the Levites were numbered from thirty years old and upward, and their number by census of men was 38,000.

Of these, 24,000 were to oversee the work of the house of the Lord; and 6,000 were officers and judges,

*And 4,000 were gatekeepers, and 4,000 were praising the Lord **with the instruments** which David **made** for giving praise* (1 Chronicles 23:1-5).

Look again at the last few words in this passage: "praising the Lord with the instruments which David *made* for giving praise" (1 Chron. 23:5b). The Hebrew word translated as "made" in this passage makes its first appearance in the Bible in the verse that says, "And God *made* [*asah*] the firmament..." in Genesis 1:7. David personally made or crafted instruments for this temple band. This word is often translated, "to create, to make, to do, to fashion."

Why am I making such a big deal over such a little word? Does it really matter? Ask yourself how often you've heard of people creating new musical instruments—quite a few have appeared in the last few decades, and most of them were linked to modern technologies in electronics or non-metal components. God was giving David new music that couldn't be produced by existing musical instruments and methods. The only solution for this psalmist was to create new instruments and methods to match the new music in his soul! Is God trying to give you new music? Are you ready for a new song and a new sound to create it?

If you are a musician, then you know exactly what I'm talking about. The scene is hauntingly familiar: Somewhere, somebody begins to say, "Oh man, if I could just get this much more out of my saxophone...my guitar...my violin...my drums...my clarinet." Suddenly we have new or modified instruments created because of a mysterious drive to express what we feel within. Today, we are blending the incredible power of technology with musical creativity to produce sounds that we thought only would be heard in our dreams or in Heaven one day.

When the Hammond organ was first introduced, it had the most profound influence on jazz and gospel music forms at the time. I'm not sure whether it emerged in both jazz and gospel simultaneously, because both of them are interlinked in certain places. When technology or human ingenuity suddenly kicks in and says, "Hey, I can give you a new sound...we'll MIDI your keyboard to this unit...," what is the typical reaction among folks in the Church?

They may say, "Well, that's certainly not of God. That's not the way my grandfather did it, and that is certainly not the way David did it." I think we might be surprised at David's reaction if he were with us today.

Step back to the time about 5,000 years ago when music and musical instruments were fairly primitive. King David began to hear new sounds during his time of praise and worship before the ark of the covenant. This consummate worshiper, musician, praiser, and psalmist also wrote, prophesied, preached, and publicly declared things to the congregation of the Lord. He did all of it out of the psalmic mode. This man of the future was hearing and seeing things in the heavenlies for which there were no earthly counterparts during his lifetime. It was up to him to bring what he saw in the heavenlies in vision and revelation back down to the earthly plane.

He must have asked himself, "How do I reproduce the sound that I heard in the heavens?" Once he had the answer, he told his son, "I want you to build this temple exactly according to the pattern God put in my mind. Now the sound I heard can't be produced the old way—forget the two-man duets for this temple. You will need to think a little bigger this time. It'll take, let's see, multiply the four, carry the zero—we'll need four thousand singers, Sol. And the old instruments can't carry this thing by themselves, but don't worry about it. God gave me some ideas and I just made up some new instruments myself! Give these instruments I made to your new holy jazz band and turn them loose to do something completely different."

What happened at David's tabernacle in the years before Solomon built the temple wasn't just a new sacrifice. God was birthing a new sound and a new song in His psalmist. Read through the Psalms and ask yourself how many of those psalms were born in the presence of God when David was seated right there next to the ark, gazing into the face of God at the tabernacle. David entered the glory of God and emerged with something new that you and I still need to receive and manifest in our day!

David prayed an astounding prayer while he was sitting before the presence of God that is preserved for us in one of his most famous psalms: "One thing I have asked from the Lord, that I shall seek: That I may dwell in the house of the Lord all the days of my life, to behold the beauty of the Lord, and to meditate in His temple" (Ps. 27:4).

This is a song that was born out of David's revelation and openness to the Holy Spirit's inward work. He was sitting in the presence of God, just listening and soaking in His glory. It was only natural that David was inspired and his heart was opened to new experiences, understanding, and creativity. Doesn't the apostle Paul tell us in the New Testament: "But we all, with unveiled face beholding as in a mirror the glory of the Lord, are being transformed into the same image from glory to glory, just as from the Lord, the Spirit" (2 Cor. 3:18)?

When God is giving birth to something new within you, when He is crafting something divinely creative in your heart, you don't say, "I don't want this creative stuff now. It's inconvenient, and I'm not sure I even believe in it." Just like natural babies often come in the middle of the night, spiritual babies may come at "inconvenient times" too, but if you are wise, you simply do what must be done to accommodate God's Presence. We have been warned by the prophet in Isaiah who said, "You will have songs as in the night..." (Is. 30:29).

Religious people need to just give up being "religious" and simply understand that when God said in Isaiah 43:19a, "Behold, I will do something new, now it will spring forth; will you not be aware of it?" He wasn't talking about a one-time event; He was describing His eternal mode of continually doing new things in the earth for His own glory.

Now, I want to say something that's going to shock you: *I don't believe all the new stuff goes to the world first.* I believe it goes to God's people *first*, but too often we say, "That isn't God," and reject it because it is new or different. But God wants to get it into the earth, and He will use whatever channel is open to Him. My Bible says, "Every good thing bestowed and every perfect gift is from above, coming down from the Father of lights, with whom there is no variation, or shifting shadow" (Jas. 1:17).

When God gives us supernatural assignments like, "Reach your generation with the gospel of Jesus Christ," then I believe He also supplies us with everything we need to accomplish our task. So we march out and try to reach our generation with the same music and language the previous generation used to reach us. The results are predictable: We sing to them, "Oh for a thousand tongues to sing..." and they smirk back at us and say, "Forget it man. Where's the beat?" We have no business trying to force-feed today's children with yesterday's meal plan. And there is no need! God gives each generation a new song and a new sound to win the world—if they only will listen and receive them!

How many times have you heard somebody say, "Rock and roll? *That's the devil's music*"? The devil doesn't have any music, because he is incapable of "creating" anything. He is a preemptor by nature and by necessity. He didn't know anything about sex, but he was able to twist sex so he could use it to fulfill his own crooked designs. God created sex and gave it to us, and the devil deviated sex and twisted it among us. God created music, and the devil distorted and misappropriated music's innate power of suggestion, reinforcement, and influence. God created art and gave it to man; the devil distorted art and uses it to mock its Creator. God created sculpture and gave it to man, and the devil distorted sculpture and used it to make idols to demons. Satan is not a creator; he is only a distorter and preemptor.

We need to pray: "O God, show us how to recover that which has been distorted. Then show us how to advance about nine steps ahead of the distorter so we can 'pied piper' a brand-new sound to lead a brand-new generation to the Savior!"

David awakened his world with such a phenomenal depth and scope of praise and worship that it literally, physically extended the borders of the Kingdom of God! Hosea the prophet wrote, "Take words with you and return to the Lord. Say to Him, 'Take away all iniquity, and receive us graciously, that we may present the fruit [calves—KJV] of our lips' " (Hosea 14:2).

If we focus on the Lord and the things He has given us, and stop thinking about the things that are going on around us, and if we begin to offer Him the fruit of our lips, notice what happens:

1. FORGIVENESS, HEALING, LOVE: "I will heal their apostasy, I will love them freely, for My anger has turned away from them" (Hosea 14:4). God says He will heal and love freely.

2. ESTABLISHMENT, FRUITFULNESS: "I will be like the dew to Israel; he will blossom like the lily, and he will take root like the cedars of Lebanon" (Hosea 14:5).

3. SENT OUT SHOOTS (EVANGELISM): "His shoots will sprout, and his beauty will be like the olive tree, and his fragrance like the cedars of Lebanon. Those who live in his shadow will again raise grain, and they will blossom like the vine. His renown will be like the wine of Lebanon" (Hosea 14:6-7).

People are hungry for God, and God is waiting for us to begin singing a new song tailor-made for our generation, complete with a new sound! Even while we are begging Him, "O God, I want to worship You," His Spirit is pleading with us: "Try something *new*. Just try. Try singing a new song to Me, a song that I will use to draw the nations." We need to humble ourselves before His tabernacle, a tabernacle not made with hands, and begin to pray together in unity:

Lord, we bring the sacrifice of praise into Your house, O God. Lord Jesus, we declare that You are the King of Kings and Lord of Lords, the Savior who is the same yesterday, today, and forever. We magnify You. We exalt You and lift up Your holy name. Make Your praise glorious in this place.

Lord, take the new sound, the new song, and the new sacrifice and move them together. Blend together that which is old and that which is new, join that which is fresh with that which is worn and familiar to us. Bring them all together in a marvelous and magnificent mosaic of worship, adoration, praise, and thanksgiving unto Your glory.

We ask that there would be times of shouting, of offering pure sacrifices of joy, and times of prostration when we bow before You and open our hearts to You.

And we ask You to speak to us. We will declare Your majesty and affirm Your right to rule the universe and our individual lives.

Most people read books in private settings where they aren't bothered by outside distractions or voices. If you are alone right now, you can still begin by praying this prayer right now in the privacy of your own prayer time:

Father God, Master and Ruler of the universe, I bow before You in this sacred moment, acknowledging Your right to receive my worship, my love, and my devotion. You paid the price: You gave Your Son. He gave His life, and today I'm here in this place because of Your grace and mercy. Open my heart to You; make me a worshiper, a lover of things fresh and new, a lover of things historic and old, to see Your treasures in all of these. I confess that Jesus Christ is Lord of Lords, King of Kings, to the glory of God the Father.

Allow the Holy Spirit to walk into your life, into every hidden closet and locked room. Invite Him into the house, and give Him free rein to rearrange furniture and priorities, adjust schedules, move out unneeded clocks, shut off the appliances, and take complete control.

Lord, make us living instruments of worship and praise, created to sing new songs and creative ever-changing melodies at Your slightest cue, and to sing majestic hymns to Your glory with awesome unique sounds emanating from redeemed vessels of praise!

Chapter 12

A New Sacrifice

Take words with you and return to the Lord
(Hosea 14:2).

A hobo walked up to a lady's house, knocked on the door and said, "Do you have a bowl of soup and a sandwich for a hungry man?"

She said, "Yes."

And he said, "Thank you."

Then the woman added, "You don't have to thank me. Do you see that pile of wood over there?"

The hobo said, "No, I don't see it."

Exasperated, the woman said to him, "I just saw you see it!"

The hobo shook his head and said, "Ma'am, you might have saw me see it, but you ain't going to see me saw it."

This is our situation, too. If you are honest (and I'm sure you are), then you have to admit that there are things you are unwilling to "see" about yourself, your situation, your family, and your prayer and worship life. Most of us think that if we say that we see it, then like the old hobo, we'll have to go "saw it." If we say, "Yes, Lord, I'm holding back in my worship because I'm afraid of what the people around me will think," then we are sure that God is going to make us do something about it. He probably will, but pretending the problem doesn't exist dooms us to continue living in the delusion of a charade and the grip of a lie.

Until David's day, the only way to communicate to God was through the sacrifice of animals and the offering of grain offerings. David broke through the barrier on the strength of the intimate relationship he forged with God during his years alone in the fields and the dark years in the cave of Adullam. The day King David sat down in front of the ark of the covenant to commune with God, a window opened in time. That window into the New Covenant revealed a glimpse of God's eternal plan to restore His intimate fellowship with man through the blood of His own Son and its natural by-product: intimacy between God and man, when "God and man at table are sat down."

David perceived there was another sacrifice that God loved more than the sacrifice of bulls, goats, and sheep. But it required a "heart after God." The ultimate blood sacrifice still would be required many generations later on the hill called Golgotha when Jesus Christ, the "son of David" and Son of God offered up His life as a ransom for mankind.

Nevertheless, David established some eternal patterns of God-pleasing worship that must be restored to the blood-washed Church in our day! The first pattern or principle has to do with the word *lavish*.

> *"Let your heart therefore be wholly devoted to the Lord our God, to walk in His statutes and to keep His commandments, as at this day."*
>
> *Now the king and all Israel with him offered sacrifice before the Lord.*
>
> *And Solomon offered for the sacrifice of peace offerings, which he offered to the Lord, 22,000 oxen and 120,000*

sheep. So the king and all the sons of Israel dedicated the house of the Lord.

On the same day the king consecrated the middle of the court that was before the house of the Lord, because there he offered the burnt offering and the grain offering and the fat of the peace offerings; for the bronze altar that was before the Lord was too small to hold the burnt offering and the grain offering and the fat of the peace offerings.

So Solomon observed the feast at that time, and all Israel with him, a great assembly from the entrance of Hamath to the brook of Egypt, before the Lord our God, for seven days and seven more days, even fourteen days.

On the eighth day he sent the people away and they blessed the king. Then they went to their tents joyful and glad of heart for all the goodness that the Lord had shown to David His servant and to Israel His people (1 Kings 8:61-66).

The sacrifices that were celebrated around the tabernacle of David, and the temple that Solomon built to David's specifications (erroneously called Solomon's temple) represented a new mode, a new way of worship. This is a new kind of sacrifice—*a lavish sacrifice.* Solomon offered 22,000 cattle and 120,000 sheep and goats. Would you say that was "lavish"? It was also lengthy. These people held continuous church services for 14 days! Now this was a *lavish* time of worship.

We shouldn't hold back anything from God either. We need to acknowledge the fact that *it takes time to worship God* the way we should. We need to set aside seasons individually and corporately just for the exclusive worship of God. If we have to take some vacation time to do it, then we need to take the time to say, "God, I'm going to give You this day. All day long I am going to worship You and focus on You alone above all things."

If you dare to set this kind of priority and make this kind of sacrifice to God, then fasten your seatbelts. No matter how hard you try, *you can't out-give God.* David tried and "failed miserably" if these verses in the Book of First Kings are a true record of Solomon's life after the dedication of the temple:

> *Now the **weight of gold** which came in to Solomon in one year was **666 talents of gold**,*
>
> *Besides that from the traders and the wares of the merchants and all the kings of the Arabs and the governors of the country.*
>
> *And King Solomon made **200 large shields of beaten gold**, using **600 shekels of gold on each large shield**.*
>
> *And he made **300 shields of beaten gold**, using three minas of gold on each shield, and the king put them in the house of the forest of Lebanon.*
>
> *Moreover, the king made a great throne of ivory and **overlaid it with refined gold**.*
>
> *There were six steps to the throne and a round top to the throne at its rear, and arms on each side of the seat, and two lions standing beside the arms.*
>
> *And twelve lions were standing there on the six steps on the one side and on the other; nothing like it was made for any other kingdom.*
>
> *And all King Solomon's **drinking vessels were of gold**, and all the **vessels of the house** of the forest of Lebanon were of **pure gold**. None was of silver; it was not considered valuable in the days of Solomon* (1 Kings 10:14-21).

Verse 27 adds a unique perspective to this picture of bounty: "And the king made silver as common as stones in Jerusalem" (1 Kings 10:27a). How do you get to that place? Offer lavish sacrifices to the Most High.

Let me ask you a simple question: "From where did Solomon reap all of this wealth?" Yes, God made Solomon wiser than any other man on earth, but according to First Chronicles 29, Solomon was really reaping from the lavish sacrifices and gifts of his father, King David, who said, "Now I have prepared *with all my might* for the house of my God the gold for things to be made of gold, and the silver for things of silver..." (see 1 Chron. 29:2).

Now when the Bible says David did something "with all of his might," then that means this man was expending Davidic-type energy! That means David was once again expending "lion-killing" energy, "bear-killing" energy, and "Goliath-killing" energy. That sounds like a guy you would want on *your side*, doesn't it?

King David didn't stop after he gathered gold and silver and other metals for the construction and decoration of the temple. He wanted to offer something *really* special to God, something that "hurt" because of its value to him personally:

*"And moreover, in my delight in the house of my God, **the treasure I have** of gold and silver, I give to the house of my God, over and above all that I have already provided for the holy temple,*

"Namely, 3,000 talents of gold, of the gold of Ophir, and 7,000 talents of refined silver, to overlay the walls of the buildings;

"Of gold for the things of gold, and of silver for the things of silver, that is, for all the work done by the craftsmen. Who then is willing to consecrate himself this day to the Lord?" (1 Chronicles 29:3-5).

King David sowed such a lavish sacrifice to God in his life that his son, King Solomon, was able to reap from the bounty of God's return on a scale that is almost unimaginable today! By my reckoning, if you add up all of the things Solomon gave away during his reign, you have to come to the conclusion that Solomon *gave away* nearly *two billion dollars* worth of gold and gifts for the Lord's service! Now that's what David, his father, sowed into the purpose of God. Who reaped a harvest from it? Solomon did.

We all need to understand something about the whole business of giving something to God: *When you give something to God, He isn't just looking at you—He is looking at your seed.* He's looking at the generation that is going to follow you!

When you bless your heavenly Father, the God from whom all blessings flow, He will not only set out to bless you, but also He will make sure He blesses your children, and your children's children after them! Don't believe the devil's lie that this kind of "generational blessing" somehow died out after the Book of Malachi, that it is strictly some kind of "Old Testament fairy tale." God isn't like mankind—He doesn't change. He's going to bless your children's children, and it will be His delight and good pleasure to do so! This point is beyond argument: God blesses those who bless Him!

Now, there is something else that we should notice about this sacrifice Solomon offered to God at David's command. Even though Solomon and the priests offered the lavish sacrifice of 22,000 cattle and 120,000 sheep and goats over an unbroken period of 14 days while the people of Israel watched and rejoiced, no one was upset over burned roast, a missed football game, or lack of sleep. They were happy and filled with joy. (Wouldn't you like to feel that way every time you leave a church service?)

Here is another important point: The *new sacrifice* David pioneered in the fields, the cave, and the "tabernacle of David" on Zion was carried over into the worship offered in the new temple Solomon had built. Many generations later, when King Hezekiah ordered that the abandoned temple be repaired and worship resumed, we still find David's "new sacrifice" observed:

Then Hezekiah gave the order to offer the burnt offering on the altar. **When the burnt offering began, the song to the Lord also began with the trumpets, accompanied by the instruments of David king of Israel.**

While the whole assembly worshiped, **the singers also sang** *and the* **trumpet sounded;** *all this continued until the burnt offering was finished.*

Now at the completion of the burnt offerings, the king and all who were present with him bowed down and worshiped.

Moreover King Hezekiah and the officials ordered the Levites to **sing praise to the Lord with the words of David and Asaph the seer. So they sang praises** *with joy, and bowed down and worshiped* (2 Chronicles 29:27-30).

This is a picture of what God wants to restore to the Church today. When David came into the presence of God, he brought a sacrifice of the lips to God. He brought words and songs of adoration, love, reverence, and awe to his mighty God. The whole idea is that God wants us to understand that *singing is its own sacrifice!* It is nowhere described more powerfully than in the Book of Hosea:

Take with you words, and turn to the Lord: say unto Him, take away all iniquity, and receive us graciously: so will we render the ***calves*** *of our lips* (Hosea 14:2 KJV).

Calves? That's right! Although most modern translations insert "fruit" in place of "calves," the older translation is more accurate! Hosea the prophet used the Hebrew word *par*, which means "a bullock (apparently as breaking forth in wild strength): a young bull, calf, ox."[1] The prophet is saying the words of our lips are equal in God's sight to the physical sacrifice of calves under the old sacrificial system.

While you begin to sing to the Lord as a blood-washed priest and king in Christ, you are offering a high sacrifice to God that is holy and acceptable in His sight. When David sat before the presence of the Lord and offered the worship of his heart and lips—even without animal sacrifice or grain offering—he was tapping into the dynamic truth that Jesus revealed when He told the woman at the well, "God is spirit, and those who worship Him must worship *in spirit and truth*" (Jn. 4:24).

Many Christians and church congregations have abandoned the dynamic power of true Spirit-led praise, worship, and the sacrifice of their lips to God. They have fallen into the rut of rote worship and of religion by the letter, when God really wants them to worship the Father in *spirit* and in *truth*. We ought to know better, but too many of us don't act like it.

Too many of us stow away the unforgettable images of ecstatic worship, humble prostration, and ear-deafening praise found in the Book of Revelation to the distant future, never realizing that this is also a picture of the emerging Church of Jesus Christ! It was Jesus who taught His disciples to pray to the Father, "Thy will be done on earth as it is in Heaven." By our actions we are praying, "Father, Thy will *will have to wait* till we finally get to Heaven!"

What have we learned about worship? Perfect worship will, indeed, come only after we have received glorified bodies unhampered by the weaknesses of the flesh, but God is teaching and preparing us *right now* by perfecting our praise and worship by His Spirit.

Worship has evolved or progressed in the Bible along with our understanding of our heavenly Father. Once Adam and Eve sinned, their intimate relationship with the Creator God was severed, and they were separated from Paradise and the presence of God by the fiery sword of the cherubim assigned to Eden's gate.

Things got worse from there. Ultimately, nearly every member of our race forgot their heritage with God, except

Noah. The flood wiped away every memory of that ancient race, except Noah and his family. The knowledge of God quickly faded from Noah's descendants until a moon-worshiper named Abram met the one true God and dared to worship Him alone. His descendants grew in their knowledge of God as He intervened and guided them from generation to generation, but their walk was still primarily a walk of fear—even under the leadership of Moses.

It wasn't until David that mankind regained an understanding of God's everlasting lovingkindness, and with this new knowledge and intimacy came a fresh understanding of sacrifice and true worship. Jesus Christ was the fulfillment of what God launched through David's life and leadership. The disciples were witnesses to God's unfolding plan as the Church was birthed in the first century.

Here we are, thousands of years later, blessed with the blood of the Lamb, the gift of the indwelling Holy Spirit, and the leadership gifts and ministry gifts God gave to His Church. We have printed the Word of God in nearly every human language. We possess a vast library of Church history describing God's faithfulness and thousands of years of unfolding revelation by the Spirit to man. Yet, God says that He must rebuild the tabernacle of David (see Amos 9:11).

We were created for His good pleasure. We were created to worship and praise God and to be conformed to the image of His Son, Jesus Christ. We were commanded to love one another so the world would know His disciples. We were commanded to destroy the works of the enemy and to preach the gospel to the world. All of these mandates find their completion and secret of success in the *sanctuary*, the dwelling place of God. Our King wants to extend the borders of His holy Kingdom in the earth—and He has chosen to use hands and hearts of flesh to do it. He expects us to conquer and do battle the same way that David did it thousands of years ago from his tent on Mount Zion, seated in the presence of God.

It is time for us to shout unto God with voices of triumph (not whimpers of embarrassment). It is time for us to offer a sweet sacrifice of praise, the fruit of our lips unto the Lord. It is time to sing aloud with songs of joy to the Lord of our salvation. It is time to dance and sing before Him with all of our strength—to dance "like David danced" so the Lord can do battle in the heavenlies on our behalf.

Since we are filled with the Holy Spirit, surely, we can begin to sing a *new song* and create a *new sound* before the Lord for His glory! Surely, we can begin to speak to that "which is not as though it were"! Surely, it is time for us to rise up in Jesus' name to bind on earth those things that He has already bound and cast from Heaven's borders, and to loose on earth those things that He long ago loosed in the heavenlies.

My wife used to let me get away with bringing her some flowers whenever I had done something to hurt her, or when I felt the need to "show" her that I loved her. At the time, she knew I had too much pride to say I was sorry or to verbalize my love. Even then, the truth was that she'd rather hear an "I'm sorry" or "I love you" than receive a dozen of the finest roses. The Holy Spirit said to her, "That's his only way to do it right now. Take the flowers." In time, I learned how to say "I'm sorry" and "I love you" and *the benefits of my new ability to speak to my beloved were wonderful*!

God wants His Church to step out of the pews and sit at His feet, close enough to whisper "I love You" in His ear. He longs to see us leap for joy over His name and faithfulness. He wants to hear a "really big band sound" in His sanctuary—a sound that will make Solomon's 4,000-member team seem like a street-corner quartet and will shake the whole earth with His glory!

God wants His people to clap their hands for joy in His Presence with such power and authority that lucifer will cower with his minions to avoid the crippling blows of God's glory raining down on the earth! He wants our shouts for joy to reverberate throughout the created world and the spirit realm with rebellion-crushing intensity and power. He wants to see our words of sacrificial praise and our worship in prostration and humility build yet another even more glorious "sanctuary" and resting place for His glory. Sometimes, He even asks us to do this in the midst of sorrow or adversity.

On Thursday, January 16th, 1986, we learned that my oldest brother and his wife had been killed. Our church was in the middle of a 40-day fast, and we felt like anything could happen. But when the tragic news came, it was emotionally devastating.

When the family members arrived in Portland, Oregon, for the home-going service, we remembered that my brother had said that he didn't want anybody singing any sad songs at his funeral. He told us, "Don't bring me flowers, because I can't smell flowers." Then he added, "Now if you just have to bring something to my funeral, then bring sweet potato pies. I love sweet potato pies. I can't eat the pies, and I can't smell the flowers, but my preference would be sweet potato pies."

Well, some folks brought him some flowers anyway, but somebody got a lot of folks to bring a total of 24 sweet potato pies to the funeral, and I'm telling you it was a joy encounter! If you had come to that meeting and hadn't seen the coffin in front of the church, you would have never guessed you were at a funeral.

It wasn't that people weren't sorrowful. We were all grieving over the untimely deaths of my brother and his precious wife, but we were busy offering sacrifices of joy to the God of resurrection. The governor of Oregon was there, along with the mayor of Portland, the district attorney, and a number of law enforcement officers. My brother had an incredible entourage attend his home-going because he had greatly impacted that city. So they were all there that day, just scratching their heads and trying to figure out what kind of meeting they were in! "Is this a funeral? I thought this guy died in the prime of his life?" They were confused because even in the face of tragic death, we were offering sacrifices—and I mean *sacrifices*—of joy to our King.

My sister was "cutting a step" and shouting and dancing to Jesus, and a lot of other folks were doing the same thing. My late brother's oldest son, Johnny, started out singing in the choir, but when they started a really hot song, Johnny just had to step down out of the choir and take a hold on the edge of the coffin. Then he just started going at it with a holy dance of joy before the Lord. And all of those visiting dignitaries were trying to say, "What is this?" Some of them looked at me and said, "What's wrong with this picture?"

You should have seen the write-up for that home-going service in the newspaper! It was a testimony to the joy of the Lord in the face of death. If Christians could just learn to offer the sacrifice of joy in every circumstance, they would discover the power and blessing of a new kind of sacrifice first pioneered by David, the man after God's own heart.

God also wants to restore to us David's understanding of the value of *lavish sacrifice*! I believe David said things like, "I want something that's going to be noisy. I want something that's going to be robust. I want something that's going to be musically excellent. I want something that's going to be so innovative and press the envelope of current technology so much that I will have to make new instruments to capture the new sounds that we must have." We need to pray the same prayer today!

God is calling us to a different dimension of praise and worship. It requires each of us to come *boldly* to the throne of grace in Jesus' name. Here I come.

I believe musicians, song writers, psalmists, and singers around the world are hearing mysterious new sounds in their spirits, but don't know what to do with them! I call them forth in Jesus' name! It is time to speak out what you hear your Father in Heaven speaking! It is time to sing out what you hear the angels in Heaven singing! It is time to create the instruments that you see and hear glorifying God in the heavenlies! It is all part of bringing God's will to pass on the earth as it is in Heaven. But this task, like any other in God's Kingdom, is a supernatural task that must be done by the Spirit of God and not by the flesh of man.

God has rebuilt the tabernacle of David in our day. Now, He is waiting patiently for a people who will come boldly to sit in His Presence bearing a sweet sacrifice of praise and worship. Every wall and veil of separation has been removed. We have free entrance to His Presence through the blood of the Lamb. God has done His part; now it is our turn.

Will we be content to rest in our pew, or kneel in His rest? There is glory awaiting us at the feet of God. There is healing in abundance for us in the light of His glory. There are blessings and joys unspeakable in store for us if we will only leave our houses and sit before Him in worship and communion. There are kingdoms to conquer and enemies to vanquish through our victorious praise and uninhibited worship. All we must do is say, "Yes." Join me. Take words with you and return to the Lord's Presence. There is a seat waiting for you right beside another King who would build God a house....

Endnote

1. *Strong's*, **calves** (H6499).

For more worship resources:

TEACHING SERIES ON WORSHIP

I Love to Worship You, Lord	$20.00
Worship Postures	$20.00
Worship Patterns	$20.00
David's Tabernacle	$20.00

MUSIC TAPES

Songs of the Season—Vol I (cassette)	$ 8.00
Songs of the Season—Vol II (cassette)	$ 8.00
Songs of the Season—Vol I & II (CD)	$12.00
Maranatha "Live" (cassette)	$12.00
Maranatha "Live" (CD)	$15.00
Maranatha "Live" (Video)	$20.00
Solid Rock (cassette)	$10.00
Solid Rock (CD)	$12.00
No One Like You (cassette)	$10.00
No One Like You (CD)	$12.00
Live Concert (cassette)	$ 8.00
I Exalt Thee (cassette)	$ 8.00

Please add appropriate shipping charges:

$ 5.00 to $10.00 add	$2.00	$50.01 to $60.00 add	$ 7.00
$10.01 to $20.00 add	$3.00	$60.01 to $70.00 add	$ 8.00
$20.01 to $30.00 add	$4.00	$70.01 to $80.00 add	$ 9.00
$30.01 to $40.00 add	$5.00	$80.01 to $90.00 add	$10.00
$40.01 to $50.00 add	$6.00	$90.01 and over, add	$11.00

If you have any questions, call or write:

Joseph L. Garlington Ministries
1111 Wood Street
Pittsburgh, PA 15221
412-244-9496 (phone) 412-244-9655 (fax)
http://www.ccop.org

Make checks payable to Joseph L. Garlington Ministries. We also accept VISA, MasterCard, American Express, and Discover.

Other

Destiny Image titles
you will enjoy reading

Destiny Image
New Releases

THE MARTYRS' TORCH
by Bruce Porter.
In every age of history, darkness has threatened to extinguish the light. But also in every age of history, heroes and heroines of the faith rose up to hold high the torch of their testimony—witnesses to the truth of the gospel of Jesus Christ. On a fateful spring day at Columbine High, others lifted up their torches and joined the crimson path of the martyrs' way. We cannot forget their sacrifice. A call is sounding forth from Heaven: "Who will take up the martyrs' torch which fell from these faithful hands?" Will you?
ISBN 0-7684-2046-6

THE LOST PASSIONS OF JESUS
by Donald L. Milam, Jr.
What motivated Jesus to pursue the cross? What inner strength kept His feet on the path laid before Him? Time and tradition have muted the Church's knowledge of the passions that burned in Jesus' heart, but if we want to—if we dare to—we can still seek those same passions. Learn from a close look at Jesus' own life and words and from the writings of other dedicated followers the passions that enflamed the Son of God and changed the world forever!
ISBN 0-9677402-0-7

THE THRESHOLD OF GLORY
Compiled by Dotty Schmitt.
What does it mean to experience the "glory of God"? How does it come? These women of God have crossed that threshold, and it changed not only their ministries but also their very lives! Here Dotty Schmitt and Sue Ahn, Bonnie Chavda, Pat Chen, Dr. Flo Ellers, Brenda Kilpatrick, and Varle Rollins teach about God's glorious presence and share how it transformed their lives.
ISBN 0-7684-2044-X

FATHER, FORGIVE US!
by Jim W. Goll.
What is holding back a worldwide "great awakening"? What hinders the Church all over the world from rising up and bringing in the greatest harvest ever known? The answer is simple: sin! God is calling Christians today to take up the mantle of identificational intercession and repent for the sins of the present and past; for the sins of our fathers; for the sins of the nations. Will you heed the call? This book shows you how!
ISBN 0-7684-2025-3

Available at your local Christian bookstore.
nternet: http://www.reapernet.com

Destiny Image
New Releases

GOD'S FAVORITE HOUSE
by Tommy Tenney.
The burning desire of your heart can be fulfilled. God is looking for people just like you. He is a Lover in search of a people who will love Him in return. He is far more interested in you than He is interested in a building. He would hush all of Heaven's hosts to listen to your voice raised in heartfelt love songs to Him. This book will show you how to build a house of worship within, fulfilling your heart's desire and His!
ISBN 0-7684-2043-1

THE GOD CHASERS
(Best-selling **Destiny Image** book)
by Tommy Tenney.
There are those so hungry, so desperate for His presence, that they become consumed with finding Him. Their longing for Him moves them to do what they would otherwise never do: Chase God. But what does it really mean to chase God? Can He be "caught"? Is there an end to the thirsting of man's soul for Him? Meet Tommy Tenney—God chaser. Join him in his search for God. Follow him as he ignores the maze of religious tradition and finds himself, not chasing God, but to his utter amazement, caught by the One he had chased.
ISBN 0-7684-2016-4

GOD CHASERS DAILY MEDITATION
& PERSONAL JOURNAL
by Tommy Tenney.
Does your heart yearn to have an intimate relationship with your Lord? Perhaps you long to draw closer to your heavenly Father, but you don't know how or where to start. This *Daily Meditation & Personal Journal* will help you begin a journey that will change your life. As you read and journal, you'll find your spirit running to meet Him with a desire and fervor you've never before experienced. Let your heart hunger propel you into the chase of your life...after God!
ISBN 0-7684-2040-7

Available at your local Christian bookstore.

nternet: http://www.reapernet.com

Other
Destiny Image titles
you will enjoy reading

A DIVINE CONFRONTATION
by Graham Cooke.

The Church is in a season of profound change. The process is sometimes so bewildering and painful that we don't know which way is up or down! Here's a book that separates truth from feelings and explains the elements involved in transition. Its prophetic revelation and deep insight will challenge your "church" mind-sets and give your heart much food for thought. This book is a must-read for all who want to know what is happening in the Church today!
ISBN 0-7684-2039-3

CORPORATE ANOINTING
by Kelley Varner.

"A body you have prepared for me" (Heb. 10:5b). We all yearn for Him, but we often look for Him in the wrong place. We cannot imagine the Christ of God really being seen in frail humanity. But the fullness of His Life and power will only be seen when He can be seen in the Corporate Man, Christ Jesus, for whom Paul said he was in travail until it came to pass.
ISBN 0-7684-2011-3

A HEART FOR GOD
by Charles P. Schmitt.

This powerful book will send you on a 31-day journey with David from brokenness to wholeness. Few men come to God with as many millstones around their necks as David did. Nevertheless, David pressed beyond adversity, sin, and failure into the very forgiveness and deliverance of God. The life of David will bring hope to those bound by generational curses, those born in sin, and those raised in shame. David's life will inspire faith in the hearts of the dysfunctional, the failure-ridden, and the fallen!
ISBN 1-56043-157-1

Available at your local Christian bookstore.

Internet: http://www.reapernet.com

When your heart is yearning for more of Jesus, these books by Don Nori will help!

ther
Destiny Image titles
you will enjoy reading

AN INVITATION TO FRIENDSHIP:
From the Father's Heart, Volume 2
by Charles Slagle.

Our God is a Father whose heart longs for His children to sit and talk with Him in fellowship and oneness. This second volume of intimate letters from the Father to you, His child, reveals His passion, dreams, and love for you. As you read them, you will find yourself drawn ever closer within the circle of His embrace. The touch of His presence will change your life forever!
ISBN 0-7684-2013-X

A PASSION FOR HIS PRESENCE
by LaMar Boschman.

Here is a book that distinguishes between the omnipresence and the manifest presence of the Lord. It assists the reader in fulfilling his quest to live in God's presence. A dimension of God's revealed presence similar to that which Adam experienced in Eden or Moses at the burning bush is available to us today.
ISBN 1-56043-704-9

THE COSTLY ANOINTING
by Lori Wilke.

In this book, teacher and prophetic songwriter Lori Wilke boldly reveals God's requirements for being entrusted with an awesome power and authority. She speaks directly from God's heart to your heart concerning the most costly anointing. This is a word that will change your life!
ISBN 1-56043-051-6

Available at your local Christian bookstore.

nternet: http://www.reapernet.com